20 Wa

Within 20 Minutes

20 Circular Rambles within 20 Minutes'
Drive of Blandford Forum

With grateful thanks to all the friends and fellow ramblers who helped to "test-walk" these circuits (you know who you are) and for all their helpful comments.

Text and photographs by Claire Smith

Editing and design by Lorna Lyons

Printed by The Minster Press, Wimborne, Dorset.

ISBN 978-1-899499-98-4

CONTENTS

Whilst every effort has been made for accuracy, signs change and ease of walking on different terrains will vary with weather. We would be very pleased to receive updates as well as suggestions for further editions at: 20walksblandford@btinternet.com

C.S.

LIST OF RAMBLES

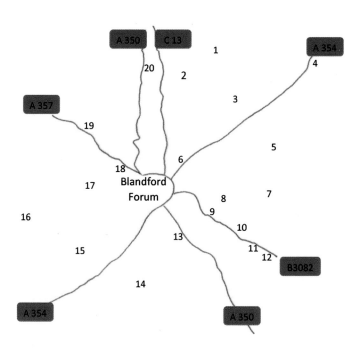

INTRODUCTION

When Daniel Defoe noted that "no town hereabouts has so large a number of gentlemen's seats" (1724) he was talking about Blandford before the Great Fire of 1731, but his comment that "the pleasant downs adjoining can hardly be equalled in the world" remains true; Location! Location! Location! There were good reasons so many rich and powerful families established country seats in the surrounding area – including principally the beauty and variety of the landscapes close to this fording-point of the Stour, so there is nowhere better placed than Blandford to access the great outdoors. The great estates of Chettle, Moor Crichel and Rushmore have different stories to tell and retain something of their ancient character.

From the north-west to the south-east run the line of hillforts of the Stour Valley; Hod, Hambledon and Badbury, still redolent of Neolithic and Roman times. To the north and the east lies Cranborne Chase and Blandford is one of its entry points. Exploring this land the walker comes upon surprises seemingly lost in time – the Dorset Cursus, a network of Roman roads such as Ackling Dyke, and Knowlton church, amongst others. It is an Area of Outstanding Natural Beauty where the chalk downland and unique landscapes were coveted for their game for many centuries. To the west lie the entrancing hills and valleys of the Winterbornes and the panoramic views of Bulbarrow, where nature and tiny villages meld into scenes of apparently tranquil beauty.

Nowadays, we can all enjoy uncovering the secrets of this area as we put on our boots and take to tracks which have been followed by our predecessors for 100's, sometimes 1,000's of years. Sunken lanes, smugglers' routes, religious houses brought down in the Tudor Dissolution, thatched cottages, old railway tracks and wonderful arched river bridges sheltering swans and herons. I have lived here for over 30 years and am still discovering, and being fascinated by, new places.

There are many other routes to choose from, but these are all close at hand, all less than 20 minutes' drive from Blandford.

HOW TO USE THIS BOOK

Each walk has a brief description followed by guidance on parking and then instructions for the route itself. There are several maps with longer or shorter versions, some of which can be done as two separate walks on different occasions.

Background and historical interest are interspersed throughout the book in red.

Where there are alternatives leading to either a longer or shorter route, these, and the arrows on the maps, are in green.

Water features are shown in blue.

The maps provided aim to give a back-up to the written instructions and have key details; they are all to scale, although the scale varies from map to map. Normal roads are shown with parallel lines, wide tracks and lanes with a single line, dashes are footpaths or bridleways and designated long-distance routes (see below) are shown by

x x ‾x· x̅‾ x— · — · — · ·   or   — · — · — · — · — · — ·

The maps and instructions aim to be as comprehensive and idiot-proof as possible, but walkers would be strongly advised to use the appropriate Ordinance Survey (OS) Explorer map, either electronic or traditional. All the walks are on footpaths, bridleways or permissive paths and are clearly marked on the OS maps. The appropriate one is suggested for each walk, but the main ones used are: 117, 118 and the Blandford Forum Centred Map (BFCM), obtainable from the Blandford TIC or the Dorset Bookshop in the Market Place.

Finally: don't forget the **Country Code**: keep to official paths, leave no litter, always close gates and when walking on roads, keep to the right in single file making yourself as visible as possible. When walking with a dog, remember they must ALWAYS be kept on lead on the road and when there is livestock in a field. (The only exception to this is if you encounter aggressive cattle; in this case, let your dog off and he/ she will be able to save him/ herself more efficiently and you can look after yourself!)

ABBREVIATIONS AND KEY TO MAPS:

HW		Hardy Way
SVW		Stour Valley Way
WR		Wessex Ridgeway
JT		Jubilee Trail
SEW		St. Edward's Way
ⓟ		Official car park
S		Start
①		Instructions
✝		Church
Keyneston Mill		Building
Hod Hill		Geographical feature
▲		Trig point
→		Route direction
→		Alternative route
		Dorset footpath
		Dorset bridleway

RAMBLE 1 – Win Green, Tollard Royal and the Larmer Tree

5 ¼ miles or 7 miles

A walk with a challenging ascent on the return up to Win Green. This is largely a there-and-back walk; out on the Hardy Way and back on the Wessex Ridgeway. The former is a long but gentle descent whilst the latter is initially along Ashcombe Bottom onto a steep climb back to Win Green. You can, of course, armed with your OS map, opt to reverse the ascent and descent. Win Green is NT, but much of the walk is through a private estate, so dogs need to be on leads where indicated. However, there is virtually no time spent on roads, all on paths. Possibility of refreshments can be found at the King John in Tollard Royal, or the café at the Larmer Tree (Easter to September) if you choose to do the Larmer Loop (please check opening times and entry charges before travelling). Maps: 118.

The trig. point amongst the clump of beech trees signifies Win Green's height of 277 metres. This is the highest point in the Cranborne Chase and the views from here are spectacular in all directions – on a good day you can see the sea and even the Isle of Wight to the south as well as Salisbury, Glastonbury Tor and Milk Hill, the highest point in Wiltshire. This area of chalk upland is an SSSI, so spring and summer bring butterflies and many rare flowers as well as birds. You are unlikely to do a walk here without seeing red kites.

GETTING THERE: Leave Blandford on the C13 (Shaftesbury Lane) and after about 6 miles take the right-hand turn to Compton Abbas Airfield. At the junction at the end of this road cross the main road (towards the Donheads) and after about 60 yards, as you go downhill, turn right onto a bumpy by-way to Win Green.

Leave the car park through the gate at the top, signed for the Wessex Ridgeway (WR).

1. Walk with the fence to the right to the stile a few hundred yards away, but at this point leave the WR and go through a double (wood and metal) gate to the right. Walk right for a few yards, then go left on a wide stony track with grass in the middle leading straight downhill. Walk downhill for about 1½ miles ignoring other tracks which join from the left and the right until, just after passing through an (open) gateway, there is a junction of routes.

2. About 100 yards below, across the grass, is a large metal gate signed for Tollard Royal. Go through and follow the path, walking along the valley floor to Tollard Royal, regaining the WR; the signage is clear. *Tollard Royal has a history going back to at least Saxon times – it was apparently owned by someone called Toli in 1050 and the manor passed through many hands until becoming the possession of the Pitt Rivers in the early 18th century. It is part of the Rushmore Estate and King John's house (also dating from the same period as the church, the 13th century) was their main seat from this date. The Larmer Tree Gardens (nearby) were laid out by General Pitt Rivers (mainly famous as the founder of modern archaeology) in the late 19th century and were a by-word for entertainment and cultural importance. Thomas Hardy himself said, on visiting a ball there, that he would have thought himself to be in Paris, so sophisticated was it. The charming buildings in the tea gardens were snapped up by the General after the Indian Exhibition in Earls Court in 1895 and nowadays they have re-discovered their joie-de-vivre as a cultural location owing to the inception of the Larmer Tree Festival each July. King John's House (originally a hunting lodge) is now in private hands but was a public art gallery in the General's time.*

3. Arrive in the village by the pond. To see King John's House and and the 13th century church, cross the road and follow the signs. You may choose to add the loop through the Larmer Tree Gardens. Just past the church and crossing the WR, take a narrow path off to the left, behind the church-yard, soon passing through a deer gate, walking through trees to a second gate.

At the end of the trees, go through a metal gate into a grassy field and cross it diagonally right, passing to the left of two separate lone trees. Having arrived at the opposite corner, turn left through a wide metal gate onto a marked track which turns right and then left before delivering you onto the main driveway into the

Larmer Tree Gardens, opposite the far end of the car park. After the buildings and next to a large double gate, turn left onto a marked footpath

through bushes and trees. As you emerge through a gate onto the same grassy field you crossed earlier, go down then up and back to the gate in the corner on the far side. Retrace your steps back to the church. **Returning to the pond, walk back again up through the valley to the** double gate (wood and metal) at the end of the grazing area.

4. This time, the return route follows the WR exactly. So turn right after the gates, walking along a wide grassy area, Ashcombe Bottom. Eventually this arrives at a track passing over a cow-grid – the signs, though small, are very clear up the drive to Ashcombe House. *There has been a house on this site since the mid 17th century. The current one is much smaller than the 18th century version and during the ownership of the Borley family (Hugh Borley died in 1993) it became very run-down, in spite of the 15-year period when the renowned photographer and designer Cecil Beaton had a lease on it (1930-1945) when he entertained many famous media stars and artists such as Dali. It was bought in 2001 by Madonna and Guy Ritchie (the latter retained it as part of the divorce settlement) and many changes have taken*

11

place subsequently, notably the addition of a shooting lake as well as many conservation measures.

5. Near the house, which isn't visible in summer, take a sign to the left onto a grassy track which initially goes gently uphill and then more steeply through trees. Stay on WR as track turns left and ultimately out of the enclosure onto open hillside, fence to the left. Carry on climbing, straight ahead. At the top, re-enter the car park through the gates and stiles from point 1.

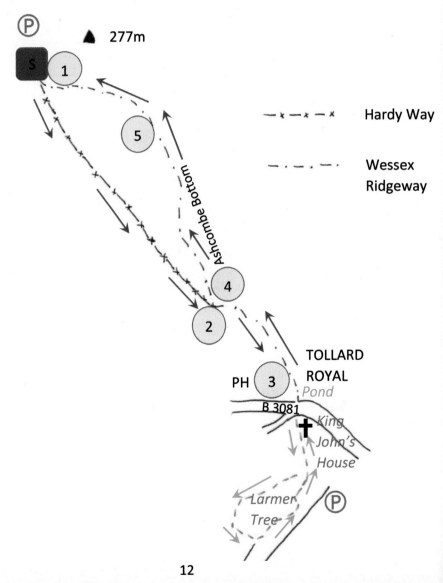

RAMBLE 2 – Ashmore and Stubhampton

7 miles

This walk starts from a high point and so there is a descent followed, eventually, by an ascent, but they are both very gentle. There is much walking under trees so good for a hot sunny day, but can be muddy in winter. Virtually no walking on roads, so good for dogs, although there are some places where dogs may have to be kept on leads. Maps: 118.

The beautiful village of Ashmore claims to be the highest village in Dorset (over 700 feet) and it is likely that there has been a village here since at least Roman times (the Badbury-Bath Roman road lies only ½ mile away) and probably the Neolithic period. Its pond, at the heart of the village, gives it a special character, being a dew pond which needs care and attention as it is 300 feet above the water table here. It is well-known locally for its midsummer festival, the Filly Loo, which takes place on the nearest Friday to the summer solstice. It takes place after dark and involves a Green Man and lots of antlers. Its origin is lost in time, indeed, it had fallen into abeyance until it was revived in 1956. It has a distinctly pagan feel to it and a wonderfully sinister atmosphere.

GETTING THERE: Leave Blandford going north on the C13, Shaftesbury Lane. After about 5 or 6 miles, take a right-hand turn marked to Ashmore. Park as near to the duck pond as possible.

Walk back along the road you arrived on. Not long after the church on your right, take a wide track (Halfpenny Lane, part of the Wessex Ridgeway (WR)) and walk along it between fields for just over ½ mile.

1. Whilst still between fields, and ignoring a first track along the side of a field, take a wide chalky track on the right, marked as a footpath, leaving the WR. Soon the track begins to go downhill between trees. At a staggered junction, go right and immediately left now with a field to the left and trees on the right. This is called Stony Bottom. Arrive at a junction with a more substantial road; do not walk on this in either direction but keep straight ahead following the bridleway sign down through the trees straight ahead.

2. At the end of this track is a junction with Stubhampton Bottom. Turn left. After a while the path bifurcates, but the two options soon rejoin; at this point, follow the bridleway sign where it veers to the right. The track soon crosses the WR, first to the right (protected path uphill) and then to the left, but go straight ahead, now with a grassy field up to the left.

3. Go through a gate and out onto a lane, still going ahead for about 100 yards then take a bridleway up towards Ashmore Barn Farm, now walking along Ashmore Bottom.

4. Leave this track where it turns left uphill towards a barn and continue straight ahead through a grassy field.

5. At end of field go through a gate and almost immediately right following a WR bridleway sign to Tollard Green. Follow track uphill through trees and at top of hill, at a junction of ways beneath a very large tree, walk right for a few yards and then take the track left between fields.

6. Soon there will be trees to the right, this is Tollard Green on the Rushmore Estate (see Ramble 3). Keep straight ahead, ignoring a bridleway right uphill. After some open fields pass through Wiltshire Coppice. Ignore any paths marked through gates to the left. When the track bifurcates, take the right fork with trees on both sides and a fence to the left. Walk between the trees for a while.

7. At junction with WR, turn left onto it, and after passing livery stables, turn right onto the lane and return to the duck pond.

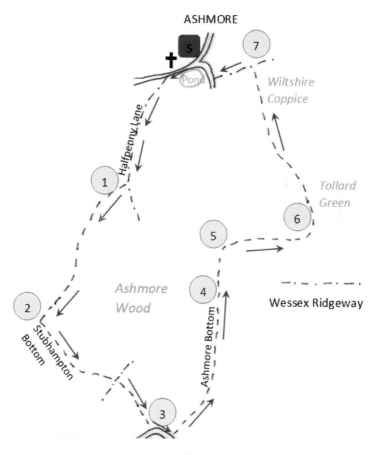

RAMBLE 3 – Farnham, Chettle and Tarrant Gunville

8 ½ miles

A longish walk but fairly easy terrain with a lot of interest. Ascents are few and gentle and there is a wide variation of route – wide tracks, some trees, several villages. Only one significant section on road so generally dog-friendly. Refreshment opportunities are Museum Inn (Farnham) and Community Shop (Chettle). Check opening hours for both. Maps: BFCM, 118.

The beautiful village of Farnham owes its present character largely to the work of General Pitt Rivers who inherited the Rushmore Estate (of which it forms part) in 1880. He was a very keen archaeologist who revolutionised the discipline by his belief in its importance lying in what it could tell us about how people in past times led their lives, rather than as individual artefacts. His collection was extensive and was open to public view in the museum which he built (now a pub/ restaurant called the Museum Inn). However, his collection outgrew the (originally 17ᵗʰ century) building and is now to be found in Salisbury Museum and the Pitt Rivers Museum in Oxford. A progressive estate-owner, he was more interested than most in the well-being and education of his workers. For them he laid out and built the Larmer Tree Gardens nearby which maintain their use and charm, and which host an internationally renowned annual festival in the summer.

GETTING THERE: Leave Blandford on the A354 towards Salisbury. After about 6 miles, pass the turning for Chettle on your left and take the next left-hand turn towards The Larmer Tree and Farnham. In Farnham, park on the road near the children's playground and telephone box (now a book swap shop).

With the play park on your left and the Museum Inn on your right, walk up the lane marked towards Chettle.

1. Pass the church of St. Lawrence on the right (with the old village well nearby) and after about 100 yards, take a footpath sign on the left with a hedge left. Then go through a gate and beside a grassy field on the left and through a gap in the hedge at the end of the second field. There is now a hedge right and an arable field left. When the track round the field turns right, go straight ahead towards an electrical substation and a line of telegraph poles.

2. At the end of the field, go through a gate marked as a bridleway, being careful of the steps, and then out onto a lane turning right.

3. After about 50 yards turn right again onto a track (the Jubilee Trail (JT), which constitutes the route as far as point 8), walking beside arable fields with the hedge to the right. Arriving at a little lane, jink right and then left, still following signs for the JT, walking between fields. At the end of the first field go through a gap in the hedge to a second field, still with the hedge left, going gently downhill. After a while, the track will narrow; there are now hedges on both sides Then head slightly uphill.

4. Soon after, come to buildings and then out onto a little lane in the village of Chettle. Turn left, passing a children's play park on the left and the Chettle Stores on the right. *Having only about 90 inhabitants, Chettle is remarkable in retaining its village shop which is very popular and much patronised locally, and just as remarkably is housed in a wartime shed from Blandford Camp. It owes much of its character to the fact that it remains a "closed" village, still owned by the Manor House. (There are only about a dozen in the country.) It has been in the hands of only two families for about 700 years. The hard times of the 18th. century delivered it into the hands of poachers and smugglers, but it survived and is now a tranquil and unique community.*

5. About 100 yards after the stores arrive at a "tree island" and turn right up towards Chettle House, the church will be on the left. A little further on, Chettle House appears behind walls to the left and away across the fields

to the right is the Castleman Arms. *The Chafin family lived in the area from at least the 16th century and Chettle House was designed by Thomas Archer and built by the Bastard brothers (of Blandford Forum fame) for George Chafin in 1710. It is a red-brick baroque house, rated by Pevsner as nationally significant and now a private house. It was bought by William Castleman in the mid-19th century who, as a railway entrepreneur, made a fortune from the Southampton-Dorchester railway, the first line in Dorset. Chettle Lodge, of a similar age, is now the Castleman Hotel and restaurant. The church dates back to the early 16th century but most of it is from a later date. However, its bells are from 1350 and it has some interesting 17th and 18th century memorials.*

When Keeper's Cottage appears to the right and a track to the left, continue straight ahead on the JT (now also the red arrow of a Public Byway) towards a metal gate and thence along a chalky track through parkland. Little Wood (originally named in estate records dating back to 935!) is to the right. After several fields pass through a metal gate, still on the JT, ignoring a right fork.

6. At a junction with a gate, go right under trees, leaving the Public Byway, but still following the JT for just over ½ mile.

7. Next, the woods on the right give way to an open field. Before the end of this field the JT turns left through a metal gate. There are JT signs on a telegraph pole before this and also on its yellow covering, but be sure not to miss it. Once through the gate, be careful to follow the angle of the JT sign, turning left along the side of the field, under telegraph wires, and then right down the second side of the field, now parallel with the telegraph poles. At a crossing with a farm track carry straight on ahead. Go through another metal gate now walking with the hedge right and parkland left. This is the edge of the parkland belonging to Eastbury House which can be occasionally glimpsed through

the trees. After the path makes a jink to the left, go through a gate into woods, still following the JT. Then a narrow path leads to a lane downhill to the "main road" through Tarrant Gunville. To get a better look at the remains of Eastbury House, go left here and then re-trace your steps.

The impressive building you can see above you is only a small part of the original Eastbury House. It was designed and built by Vanbrugh for George Dodington and at the time it was rivalled by only Blenheim and Castle Howard. It took 21 years to build, being finished in 1738. He must have been an 18th century oligarch and although "riche", definitely "nouveau". (He was a paymaster in the Royal Navy). He failed to live to see it completed and it was inherited by his nephew who was somewhat louche and a member of the Hellfire Club. He had pretensions to grandeur and entertained many eminent persons at Eastbury, including Voltaire. But after his death, no-one wanted the house, it was far too big and the next owner had it dismantled. He, however, was diddled out of the money gained by selling off the stone and fixtures and on being caught out his steward, William Doggett, committed suicide. The building you see now was the stables and kennels. Indeed, it was at one time lived in by the famous huntsman James John Farquharson whose ancestors still own it.

8. During the winter, the River Tarrant will be a stream trickling down the right-hand side of the road. Turn right up the lane.

9. Go past the new village hall, pass China Lane and take a stony right-hand track by Marlborough Farm. This soon becomes grassy. Walk along this for a while, gently uphill to a T-junction.

10. Turn left here.

11. After about 200 yards, where there are several open metal gates, turn right onto a track, hedgerows on both sides. Soon, pass a metal gate and carry on. Then gently downhill, and at Hatt's Coppice a track joins from left;

ignore it and continue straight ahead. Pass New Barn on the right and continue ahead along the lane.

12. Just before stepping out onto Dunspit Lane, turn left onto a public bridleway by a fingerpost, going downhill and then uphill.

13. At the top of the field, where the track veers left, turn right along the side of the field with the boundary on the left. (Chettle Down). There is no signage here. After completing the first side of the field, look carefully for a gap in the hedge which is your route (may be a little overgrown here for about ¼ mile).

14. Turn left onto a lane by a cottage and continue in same direction, passing an open barn on the right, uphill. (To the right, behind the trees, is Hookswood House yet another 16th/ 17th century manor house.)

15. Arrive at a road in Newtown. Turn right along the road.

16. After passing a couple of houses take a left-hand turn into a field on a public footpath and carefully follow the diagonal across the field. At the far side, cross the stile and go down to meet the lane. Turn right, down into Farnham and rejoin your car.

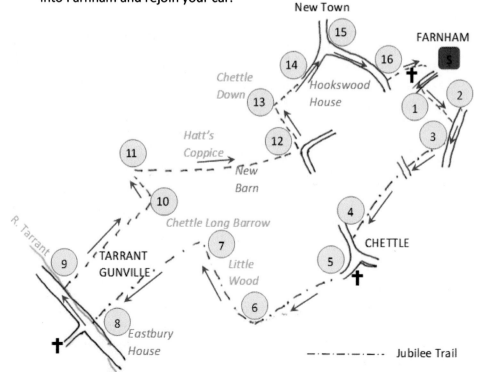

RAMBLE 4 – Pentridge and Martin Down

6 ¼ miles (possibility of 1 mile shorter)

A generally even walk, with one ascent and descent over chalk grassland grass and tracks. Only a very short distance on a lane, so good for dogs. No refreshments on route (although possibility of a van in Woodyates layby), but a picnic on Martin Down or up on the knoll is glorious. Lane past Manor Farm is often very muddy in winter.

This is a most beautiful walk in the Cranborne Chase Area of Outstanding Natural Beauty and the views across this landscape which bear the signs of human habitation since Neolithic times are all around you. You have already crossed Ackling Dyke, the Roman road which ran from Badbury to Salisbury, and the first part of your walk takes you along Bokerley Dyke (and ditch). This was built and gradually added to by a local Durotriges tribe (Celts) in the 4th and 5th centuries, following the departure of the Romans in order to protect themselves from marauding Saxons. More recently it was used by the War Office for training in WW2 and the mound and shooting range (looks like a grassy paddling-pool) are easily spotted. As a nature reserve it is host to a vast range of plants, birds and butterflies (as well as adders) which characterise unimproved chalk grassland.

GETTING THERE: Leave Blandford on the A354 towards Salisbury. After crossing the B3081 (about 9 miles) at the Sixpenny Handley roundabout, continue for a short distance. After passing the border with Hampshire and a large layby on the left at Woodyates, look out for the car park on the right, brown-signed to Martin Down Nature Reserve. There is a height-limiter at the entrance, so higher vehicles should use the lay-by previously mentioned and walk along the road to find the starting-point. Park at the furthest point from the entrance.

There are several tracks from here onto Martin Down, but take the one to the right of the information boards; within a few yards you are walking on a wide grassy path with the ditch and dyke to your right.

1. Soon, come to a tumulus like a flattened trapezium; walk to the right of this. When confronted by a short hedge facing you, take the left-hand track and carry on (if you come across an information board you have gone to the right). The path veers to the left going gently downhill. Follow this path for about a mile as far as the junction with the Jubilee Trail (JT) which crosses your path at right angles after a short descent between hedges. There is a reserve sign immediately to the right and the JT sign is about 20 yards further on.

2. Turn right onto the JT (Forde Abbey 90 miles). This is a track with a strip of trees to the left and a field to the right. Ignoring a track which joins from the left, carry on, until the track ends. Continue on the JT continue ahead, through a gate, round the side of a field, with a fence to the right.

3. At the end of the field, still following the JT, cross a stile, following the direction shown around the bottom left edge of the field. Soon, start going

uphill towards the ridge, still following the edge of this enclosure. (Ignore a JT sign which appears to lead off to the left.)

4. At the top of the field is a gate on the left which is an exit from the SSSI; don't go through it but continue to follow the fence-line, now turning to the right with Penbury Knoll ahead. This lightly wooded area has wonderful views down towards Pentridge and over Martin Down, so wander through it at will, but the actual path skirts the left-hand boundary. (If at this point you want to shorten your walk, make your way up to the trig point and over the top, picking out the route downhill over a grassy field till you come out in the village street where you turn right and rejoin the main route between 6 and 7. This avoids the muddiness of the lane to Manor Farm). As the trees grow sparser, go through a gate with a radio mast up ahead and continue ahead along the ridge.

5. Just before the Manor Farm SSSI exit turn sharp right and follow a track downhill. Pass through a gateway with a Hardy Way (HW) sign on it. Carry on ahead to the bottom of the hill.

6. Go through a gate marked HW and turn right towards the buildings of Manor Farm. Soon the track turns into a proper road approaching the village. *Pentridge has a very long history, at least as early as the 8th century and its name derives from two celtic words "pen" and "twrch" meaning "hill of the wild*

boar". It is only just in Dorset (your car park at Martin is in Hampshire, and Wiltshire isn't far either). The current St. Rumbold's church, however, dates from 1855, but can boast memorials to Robert Browning's grandparents and a WW2 RAF fighter ace who was, later as a test-pilot, the first man to fly supersonically. Pentridge figures in the works of Thomas Hardy as "Trantridge" and is where Tess comes to visit her rich aunt. There is a bridleway between here and "Chaseborough" (Cranborne) and it was on this very track (now part of the Hardy Way, of course) that the dastardly Alec d'Urberville rapes the young Tess after a visit to a dance on a Saturday night. Presumably things have changed somewhat since Hardy's time as he describes the inhabitants of Trantridge/ Pentridge as hard drinkers who were reluctant to save their money!

Just after Pembury Cottage a road comes in from the left; ignore it and carry on along the lane which leads to Whitey Top Lodge and Farm.

7. Just before the farm, where the road runs out, turn left along a grassy track between hedges. At a junction of routes at field-ends, continue to go straight ahead through a gate, following a bridleway through a field with the fence on the left. At the end of the left-hand field is an ash tree with several bridleway markers (difficult to see when the trees are in leaf). Ignore the track off to the left and continue ahead, still with the field boundary to the left. At the corner of the field, follow the boundary round to the right and in about 150 yards arrive at a gateway in the fence where there are some bridleway signs.

8. Go through it and turn left onto a grassy track back towards the car park, orienting yourself by reference to the trapezium-shaped tumulus from earlier and retrieve your car.

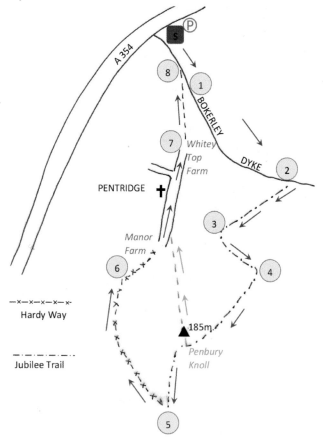

RAMBLE 5 – Gussage All Saints and Wimborne St. Giles

8 ¼ miles (+1 mile for Knowlton)

Although fairly lengthy, this is an easy-going walk on mainly wide tracks with beautiful views over Cranborne Chase. The route ascends uphill along Ackling Dyke to Harley Down, but it is very gentle. There are several sections on lanes, but there is little traffic so in general it is good for dogs. It is very varied in its interest and takes in two interesting Chase villages. For refreshment there is the Drovers' Inn at the start, and plenty of good picnic places. There is also a (well-hidden) community shop between ⑨ and the church (check all opening times before walking). Maps: 118.

There are three "Gussages", Michael, Andrew and All Saints. Gussage is an amalgamation of two Saxon words which refer to water bursting out, owing to the source of the River Allen. All Saints church has many 19th century refurbishments, but its foundation dates from the 12th – 13th centuries with a slightly later tower. It has five bells, three of which are pre-Reformation.

GETTING THERE: Take the A354 to Salisbury for about 6 miles then just past the turning to Chettle on the left turn right towards Horton. Take either the first or second turning left to Gussage All Saints and park in the main street near the Drovers' Inn (closed Mondays).

Take the grassy path at the side (right) of the Drovers' for about 100 yards.

1. Turn left along a track, walking behind the houses with a field to the right. At the end of the field continue past Manor Farm on the right and out onto the wide track, Harley Lane. (If you prefer to visit the church you can walk along the main street parallel to the footpath instead, turning right up Harley Lane after the church). After about a mile, ignore a track off to the left (which goes into a field) and walk on for several yards to a proper crossroads.

2. Turn left onto a grassy track between hedges and at the end, turn right onto another track (there aren't really any other choices). Continue along this track as it winds left past Burtt's Harley Wood and finally follow a footpath through a gateway into a flower meadow, walking along the side of the field with the hedge to the left.

3. Turn right onto Ackling Dyke, the Roman road from Sarum (Salisbury) to Durnovaria (Dorchester) via Badbury Rings. *Currently there is a 22-mile stretch which runs from Salisbury to Badbury. Originally, it was extremely wide, about 40 feet, and probably built so large to impress the local Celts. The fact that its traditional arrow straightness cuts straight through many ancient barrows and tumuli as well as the 6-mile long Dorset Cursus gives a good idea about how sensitive the Romans were to indigenous populations in conquered*  *territories.* After the pasture to the right, pass beneath trees and at the end of a rise is a crossroads with the Jubilee Trail (JT). On the left, tucked inside the field-edge is the gravestone of John Ironmonger, the agent to the Cranborne estate. This is Harley Gap. *(Take a few steps along the JT to the left and as you look out over Gussage Hill/ Down you can see tumuli and long barrows on both sides of the hill).*

4. Turn right here onto the JT and continue to a T-junction, still on the JT. From Harley Down there are excellent views over the downs to the left.
5. Turn left at this junction, still on the JT and walk downhill along the track, ignoring any exits on either side, to the lane at Monkton Up Wimborne.
6. Turn right down the road, for just over half a mile. *Here, you are as close as you can get on the surface to the source of the River Allen. There have also been significant Neolithic excavations here.*

7. At North Barn Farm take the JT sign left towards farm buildings and very soon head into the trees to the right still following the JT signage, now on a grassy track with trees uphill.

8. At the end of the track turn right onto Bottlebush Lane, now on the Hardy Way. Just after the Manor House on the right, turn left into a lane.

9. Now approaching the edge of Wimborne St. Giles; when some houses come into view on the left, take a footpath to the left and follow it past some housing, over several cross-tracks, until at the end it leads through a gate onto a playing field with a school sign. Carry straight on ahead with the hard-play area on the right to a gate and come out onto the main village street with the church opposite. Turn right through the village, over the bridge over the Allen and continue on the road climbing gently. *Wimborne St. Giles owes its existence to the manor of St. Giles, the seat of the Earls of Shaftesbury since the 17th century. St. Giles House dates from 1650 and the Almshouses (originally destined for 11 poor widows) from 1624. The church is originally Georgian (built by the Bastard brothers who re-built Blandford following the Great Fire of 1731) but largely rebuilt in the early 20th century following fire damage. The earldom of the Ashley-Cooper family was procured by judicious side-changing during the mid-seventeenth century . The seventh Earl is the most well-known, so involved was he with social reform (Factory Acts, Ragged School Movement, for example) and legislation in the interests of women and children, that Eros in Piccadilly Circus is a memorial to him; Eros' arrow is pointing in the precise direction of Wimborne St. Giles where he is buried. The ninth Earl wisely married a Grosvenor heiress which enabled much-needed renovation and modernisation of the estate. After WW2, however, 2/3 of the estate land was gradually sold off for death duties. The tenth Earl was a great lover of music and nature and made some attempts at renovation in the 1970's, but is, unfortunately, chiefly remembered for being murdered by his third wife.*

10. After St. Giles Workshops on the left go over a stile (also on the left) onto a grassy track marked with a footpath sign. Soon, arrive at an arable field and go straight ahead across the field, following a visible route (the shortest distance) to a meeting of field boundaries. At the end of this first field continue to follow the footpath sign diagonally left into another field, now walking with trees to the left and the field to the right. At the end of second field, at another junction, go straight ahead, the only non-private option, along a wide track. After passing Brockington Cottages on the right, look over the fields to the left for the first glimpse of Knowlton Church.

Knowlton is unique in its long history; this has been a sacred site for the best part of 4000 years. It is more properly known as a henge and it has become clear through excavation that this small area has been the venue for sacred activities from pagan times and then on into the Christian period. The ancient henge, taken together with the many round barrows and the 6-mile long Dorset Cursus which is now believed to have had a ceremonial function, point to this part of Cranborne Chase being one of the most sacred in the country. The particular nature of the Chase as a royal hunting ground for many centuries probably explains why so much of this whole area has been undisturbed for so long. The ruined church is Norman and dates from the 12th century. Its original village was deserted in medieval times (probably due to the Black Death) and fell into dis-use, its roof falling in in the 18th century. In common with several other sites in the Chase, Knowlton is a designated "Dark Skies" site, a result of the protection it enjoys through being in an Area of Outstanding Natural Beauty.

11. **Turn left onto Lumber lane to pass Brockington Farm.** (To visit Knowlton Church, continue down Lumber Lane for about half-a-mile to the English Heritage site and then retrace your steps.) **After about 100 yards turn right onto a stony track which soon becomes grassy (HW) with some houses to the right, and then follow a footpath sign so as not to enter a field but a narrow track between trees.**

12. At the end of the track, turn right onto the lane and walk uphill. Soon, arrive at the road junction at Amen Corner. Go straight ahead into Gussage All Saints and back to your car at the Drovers'.

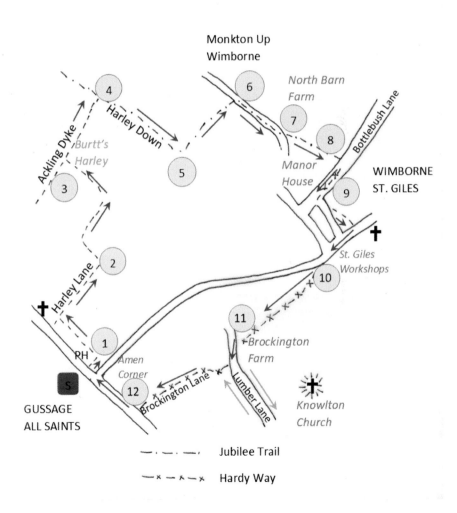

Monkton Up Wimborne

North Barn Farm

Bottlebush Lane

Harley Down

Ackling Dyke

Burtt's

Harley

Manor House

WIMBORNE ST. GILES

St. Giles Workshops

Harley Lane

Brockington Farm

Knowlton Church

GUSSAGE ALL SAINTS

Amen Corner

Brockington Lane

Lumber Lane

PH

— · — · — Jubilee Trail

—x — x — x   Hardy Way

RAMBLE 6 – Pimperne
5 ½ miles

This is a gentle walk at the edge of Cranborne Chase with fine views over the countryside. Much of the walk is on tracks and round arable fields so good for dogs. No refreshments on route but two pubs on main road. Maps: BFCM, 118.

Pimperne as a village dates from at least Saxon times and has an entry in the Domesday Book. At one time the manor was in the gift of the Crown and Henry VIII gave it to his fifth wife, Katherine Howard, who did not, of course, keep it for long and it subsequently passed into the hands of wife number six, Catherine Parr. Indeed, Queen Catherine's Walk has been a feature of the village since this time and runs through the Rectory garden. Until the early 1920's most of the village (and much of Blandford) was owned by Lord Portman and it was only when the estate was broken up and sold in 1924 that local people were able to buy the farms where they had previously been tenants.

GETTING THERE: Leave Blandford on the A354 towards Salisbury. Within a mile arrive in Pimperne. Just after the Farquharson Arms on the right take left turn to Stourpaine and Village Hall. Follow round past the church then right turn signed to Village Hall (or park in the road adjacent if you prefer).

On leaving Village Hall car park walk left, back down towards church.

1. Take the second left, Arlecks Lane, and walk uphill to a road junction. Going straight ahead, carry on up the road through the rusted white gates of the stud farm and carry on uphill for about ½ mile to the end of the metalled road.

2. Here, the route turns left in front of a hedge along a grassy track, but to see the Long Barrow, go straight ahead through a field with the hedge on your left. At the end of the field go through a gate and on the other side climb a grassy slope to stand on top of the barrow. Then return across the field and continue along the grassy track with the hedge on your right.

Pimperne Long Barrow is one of the largest in the country but it has never been excavated, so we do not know whether this is the last resting place of a single individual or many more. It was constructed around the time of Stonehenge (about 4,000 years ago) and probably took several hundred years to complete.

Pass through two fields with Ferns Plantation on the left. Continue straight ahead uphill, now with Pimperne Wood on the right. At the end of the wood come to a crossroads.

3. Turn left onto the Jubilee Trail (JT) for the next few miles. Continue downhill, with high hedges initially on both sides and through a field with the boundary to the left. At the bottom corner of the field turn left downhill through trees at Fox Warren. After about 100 yards bear left, with trees on the right and a grassy bank to the left, until arriving at Keeper's Lodge.

4. Carry straight on, down a rough track, now with trees to the left and a field on the right to a metalled road. Continue ahead to a junction with a wooden fingerpost.

5. Here, take a sharp 60 degree turn to the right, continuing along the JT and ignoring the sign back to Pimperne. Go up the wide stony track to the top of the hill.

6. Turn left into a field, still marked as the JT, which is a track cut across arable fields undulating over Pimperne Down. Continue straight ahead over two cross-tracks to a gate into some trees. The JT goes through this small woodland for about 300 yards, but if it is too overgrown, walk along the side of the field instead.

7. At the end of the trees is a junction with a minor road, Bushes Road; leave the JT which turns right. *If you would like to see the site of the Iron Age settlement (dating from about 500 BCE) which was excavated in the early 1960's, follow the Jubilee Trail sign up the road to the T-junction. This settlement straddled what is now the main road to Stourpaine, but you will have to use a bit of imagination here as everything has been covered over again. The remains of the circular timber house which was an impressive 42 feet across, however, were used as the basis for the experimental Iron Age settlement recreated at Butser Hill Ancient Farm Project near Petersfield in Hampshire (worth a visit if you are in the area). The artefacts unearthed at the time are on display in the Museum of East Dorset in Wimborne.* Turn left downhill passing Manor Farm on the left until the road bears left.

8. At this point, on the right, there is a choice of three fields; enter the middle one and walk down the left side of the field. At the bottom, look for a gate in the hedge at the end of the field. Walk down through the churchyard and out onto Church Road again.

9. Turn left to retrieve car.

   It is not known how long there has been a

church on this site; all that can be sure is that the Norman one dated from the 12th century. However, the fashion for rebuilding churches in the 19th century led to a "new" one being built by Lord Portman in 1873. He did, however retain several features from the earlier church such as the zig-zag decoration incorporated in the chancel arch on the north side of the choir, the font (though not its Gothic lid) and the doorway to the porch from the south aisle. This church is considerably larger then the Norman one but still retains the 15th century perpendicular tower. The church's registers go back to 1559, (although the requirement for parishes to record details of baptisms, marriages and burials dates from Thomas Cromwell's vice-regency in 1538, following the inception of the Church of England in 1534). Its lychgate, though, is a recent addition, given to the church by the Woodhouse family (see Ramble 16) in the late 1940's in memory of their family members who had perished in the two World Wars. Outside the gate you will find the 14th century preaching cross used by friars who were forbidden use of church buildings at that time. It was also the site of the medieval wooden pillory (abolished as a form of punishment in 1837 but not removed intil 1907).

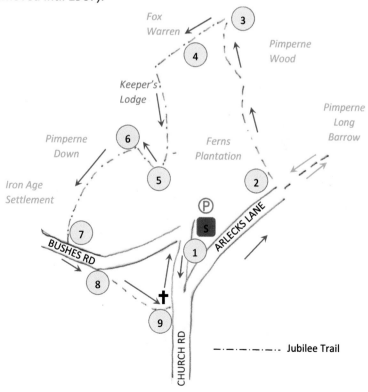

RAMBLE 7 – Witchampton and Moor Crichel

3 miles or 6 miles

Both versions of this walk have aspects to recommend them, but the longer one gives more idea of the individual character of the estate of Moor Crichel. Both routes are mostly flat and generally good for dogs as there are paths but no fields. No refreshments en route but lovely picnic places beside the River Allen. Community Shop in Witchampton. Maps: 118.

The beautiful and unusual character of Witchampton is a result of its being an entirely owned village of the Crichel Estate until the mid 20th century. There was a Roman settlement at Hemsworth just west of here where excavations uncovered a mosaic pavement showing Venus arising from her shell (so Botticelli didn't get there first!) now in the British Museum and certainly a Roman vineyard adjacent to the church. The Museum also has a set of 5-inch high chess pieces dating from the 11th century. The church is largely Victorian with a 15th century tower and 13th century font (bowl) previously used as a cattle trough. The oldest house is the Abbey House but the name is mis-leading.

GETTING THERE: Leave Blandford on the B3082 towards Wimborne. After a mile or so, at the top of the hill, turn off left at the golf course. Carry on downhill to the end of the road, then turn left. About ¼ mile after Rawston Farm take a right hand turn steeply uphill to Witchampton. Follow this road to the village centre and park either in a lay-by near the church or in the main road near the village club and shop.

Carry on walking along this road (away from shop) to Lawrence Lane.

1. Just after this go through the estate entrance on your left, walking on the Hardy Way (HW). *As you pass the cricket pitch, look straight ahead of you for the best view you will have of Crichel House. The original Tudor Manor was burnt down in 1742 and rebuilt, largely by John Bastard and Frances Cartwright of Blandford, but then re-modelled and greatly enlarged by Humphrey Sturt who inherited it in 1765. This was when he decided that every estate owner needs a lake, so he dammed the River Allen to create one. Unfortunately, this was where the estate-workers lived so they lost their homes and were moved further afield to what is now Newtown (adjacent to the site of the mills). Its notoriety came about owing to the Crichel Down Affair – a long-lasting court case finally decided in the 1960's when the Marten family sued the*

government following the compulsory purchase of a part of the estate following requisition during WW2 and afterwards. The house had a short existence as a girls' boarding school and the major part of the estate was bought by an American billionaire in 2013.

2. Soon after the cricket ground the path takes a right-hand turn, trees to the left and a field to the right. Continuing under trees there are soon encounters with the River Allen which flows into Wimborne where it is a tributary of the Stour. Ignore any tracks off to the side of this one, going ahead over an old stone bridge, staying on HW till point 4.

3. After about a mile come to a T-junction at Didlington Farm by a large barn and brick house. Turn left for the longer walk (the signage is lacking here but there is a HW sign a bit later on), towards Stanbridge. Continue past Didlington Mill and a white cottage left.

    For the shorter walk, turn right here, following a track between fields. After about ½ mile, about half-way along the third field, there is an unmarked but easily discernible track across the field on the right. Follow this, then go over a stile under trees with the Allen's backwaters around, along a protected grassy path behind and beside houses. Finally, cross a small bridge and after about 50 yards out onto the road.

     *As you cross the bridge, look down the river and the large white house with wrought-iron (on the right) is the last vestige of the Witchampton Mills, the Mill Manager's house. There were flour mills here in Saxon times which in 1720 were re-built as paper mills. By the 1960's they were no longer economic and in 1993 they were pulled down and replaced by housing, although several old "ruins" remain.* Walk right, up through Newtown to the gates where you entered at 1. Carry on ahead and retrieve car.

    After a while, the track takes a sharp left across the river again.

    The next building is Crichel Mill where the track climbs uphill between fields towards Mill Hill Wood. Carry on through the trees to a junction at Mill Hill Lodge and a signpost showing Horton right and Witchampton acute left. Leave the Hardy Way.

4. Go towards Witchampton and walk through the allée of beech trees. Going downhill, catch a last glimpse of Crichel House with its private chapel ahead and to the left. Carry on along this road for about ½ mile until the road goes sharply left.

5. Carry on straight ahead to Cock Crow Farm, on a no-through road.

6. Arriving at the farm gate follow the bridleway sign ahead into the yard and down the forest track to Manswood. Follow this wide track down through Oakhills Coppice, ignoring a track leaving to the right, to a meeting of ways between fields where there is a bench to the right (thoughtfully supplied for picnicking). Veer left with trees and hedge to the left and a field to the right for about 60 yards. Where this wide track turns right down the second side of the field, carry on straight ahead on a narrow track between trees. Soon, pass a row of brick-built cottages (the Buildings, Manswood). At the end of this row, follow the lane round to the right and down to a crossroads.

7. Cross the road *(in front of you the interesting building was once the Village Hall and School but is now in private hands)* and continue along bridleway (Rowbarrow Lane).

8. Just after Hilda Cottages, come to a road and turn left. Follow this road (Sheephouse Drove) down the hill, past Downley Coppice on the left to a junction.

9. Here, do a jink across the road following the sign saying Witchampton ¼ mile, back into the village and the car.

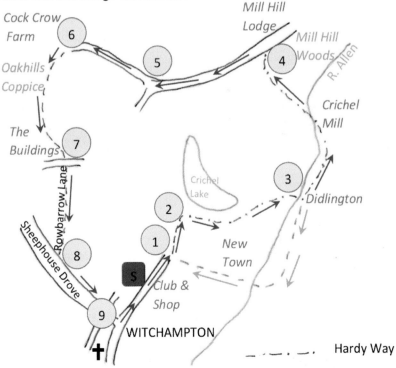

RAMBLE 8 – Tarrant Rushton Airfield

8 miles

A walk that takes in some interesting WW2 and aviation history, easy-walking tracks through farmland and a corner of the Moor Crichel estate (see RAMBLE 7). Apart from the first few hundred yards, mostly flat and very little on roads so suitable for dogs. A large part of the route very open, so probably best avoided on hot days. No refreshments on route, but Langton Arms at Tarrant Monkton (about 5 minutes away) and True Lover's Knot (see below). Maps: BFCM, 118.

The River Tarrant (meaning "trespasser" as it so frequently overflowed its banks) is a rare chalk stream which gives its name to 8 villages along its 12-mile length as it flows into the Stour at Tarrant Crawford. St. Mary's church, Tarrant Rushton, is a beautiful little church. It was consecrated towards the end of the 12th century and some Norman features still remain. Renovated in Victorian times, it is still recognisably medieval with additions and is well worth a visit. It also boasts a "lepers' squint" which allowed members of the nearby colony to participate in church services.

GETTING THERE: Blandford on the B3082 towards Wimborne. After about 3 miles, turn left at True Lovers' Knot. After ¾ mile turn right over a narrow bridge over the Tarrant to Tarrant Rushton and follow the road up the hill and park near the church. (If parking area full, continue up the hill and park on road).

On leaving the car re-trace steps back out onto the road and walk uphill for about 400 yards to gate at entrance to old airfield. Go through left-hand gate. The concrete paths were part of the old runways and adjacent roads.

1. Turn left onto this wide path walking between arable fields. In the distance rises the tower of Blandford Camp to the left. After just over a mile following the curve of the path, ignoring tracks off to the side, arrive at a large barn.

2. Turn left at this point to arrive at Windy Corner, site of the memorial to the WW2 RAF and SOE. Go through a gate out onto the road and walk right along it for about 700 yards.

The large barn is all that is left of the extensive buildings and towers which were here in WW2. Take a moment to stop and look at the memorial; in 2019 the Wimborne RAFA held a 75th Anniversary Service here. In the exhibition in the Pegasus Bridge

Museum just outside Caen, there are photos of whole phalanxes of gliders and aircraft drawn up on this airfield prior to D-Day in 1944. Indeed, the earliest airborne troops into the Battle of Normandy set out from Tarrant Rushton airfield on the night of 5th June, 1944. The airfield was also instrumental in the battle of Arnhem and in supplying materials and SOE personnel to the French Resistance. There were 3 runways here and the steep-sided valley was a great help to the gliders taking off. Post-war, the airfield was taken over by Sir Alan Cobham and Flight Refuelling which not only flew 1000's of sorties out of here for the Berlin Airlift in 1948-49, but was where they developed their revolutionary air-to-air refuelling techniques. It was last used in 1980.

3. Cross the road and go through a gate onto a concrete track. Passing a thatched cottage on left, continue along the track and up a slope. Ignore two tracks off to the right and continue to a T-junction, about 600 yards.

4. Turn right onto a stony track, initially with trees on both sides. Follow it round as it turns right when arable fields appear left, giving beauttiful views over the Tarrant valley. Another ½ mile to a junction of tracks, go right. At the next junction (about ¼ mile), take another right-hand fork. Walk for about a mile, passing an open-sided barn on the right to the next junction of tracks; ignore the one to the left and carry straight on.

5. Arriving at Dean Farm take the right of way (rightish) for about 50 yards across a field and pass through a gate onto a track between high hedges. *The attractive farm buildings date from the late 17th century with additions in the 18th.*

6. After a couple of hundred yards the bridleway crosses the road. Go through a metal gate along the bridleway through the Hemsworth Estate. Follow the main track as it bends this way and that, ignoring any side tracks. At a little island of trees, ignore the track to the left, but go straight ahead between fields with a hedge on the right.
    Hemsworth Farm and barn are grade II listed buildings dating from the 16th century but with many later additions, particularly in 19th. You are now in the parish of Witchampton which was in private hands (the Crichel Estate) until the mid-20th century, which may account for the persistence of these venerable rural buildings. Away to the right were found the remains of a Roman villa and also a vineyard. (See Ramble 7).

7. After passing a modern barn on the left, soon rejoin the concrete paths of the airfield and go left. Passing a woodchip plant, continue along this path.
8. At a large manure dump (at the time of writing), take the right-hand fork, soon passing and ignoring a footpath through Preston Farm on the left.
9. Eventually, pass a small strip of trees on the right and soon after approach the gate where you entered the airfield. Pass back through the gate, down the hill and retrieve car.

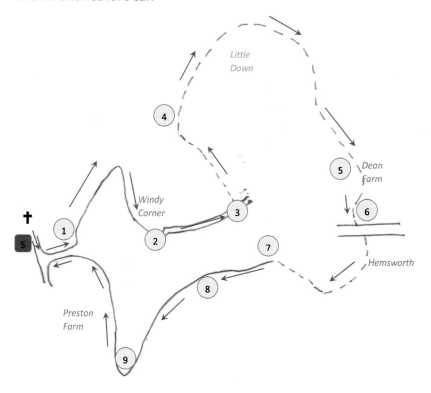

RAMBLE 9 – TARRANT MONKTON

4 miles

Easy walking, no stiles, no cows. Very good for dogs as mostly on tracks with very little on roads. Refreshment possibility at Langton Arms (or True Lovers' Knot nearby). Maps: BFCM, 118.

Tarrant Monkton, with its ford (locally called the Splash) and thatched cottages is a most attractive village which lies within the Cranborne Chase Area of Outstanding Natural Beauty and is also popular on account of its pub/ restaurant The Langton Arms. It is one of eight villages which descend the River Tarrant, a chalk stream. (There only about 200 of these known globally and 85% are in England). Next to the ford (at the end of your walk) is a 16th century packhorse bridge, one of the few remaining in Dorset. All Saints' church where you are starting your walk has parts – the chancel, the nave and the tower – which date back to the 15th century, although like many churches in Dorset it was extensively renovated in Victorian times.

GETTING THERE: Leave Blandford on the B3082. After a mile or so, at the top of the hill, turn off left at the golf course. Carry on downhill to the end of the road, then turn left, finally taking a left-hand turn signposted Tarrant Monkton. Park next to the church in the centre of the village near the Langton Arms.

With the church behind you, turn right and walk back along the lane through the village.

1. After about 400 yards, after passing a house called Riverside on the left, turn left and cross the bridge over the Tarrant, Manor Farm to the right.

2. At the end of the lane cross the road at a T-junction and almost immediately take the stony track uphill between hedges next to Guppy's Cottage (Common Drove).

3. At the end of the track, where it widens out, stand on the top of the ridge, turn round and see the Tarrant Valley stretching out beneath you. At this T-junction turn right past a vehicle gate, now walking along Little Down between hedges and fields with some woodland appearing later on the left.

4. After about half a mile, face trees at the end of this track. Turn left with a field to the left and trees to the right. After about 80 yards go through a gateway next to a metal fence. Carry on straight ahead ignoring the entrance to a field on the right. Soon there are trees on both sides and a field opens out on the left.

5. At the end of the field is a junction with a bridleway. Turn left along this wide stony track, a field left and woods right. The track dips down and then gently goes back uphill again. Ignore tracks coming in from right and then left and continue to a crossroads.

6. Turn left here, climbing gently uphill with fields right and trees left. This is Launceston Wood and in spring and early summer it is alive with birdsong. Ignoring tracks off to the right and left, continue uphill.

7. At the top of the hill lies a junction with another track. Up to your right you can see the embankment of a reservoir, but turn left onto the track between trees. Away in the distance is the tower of Blandford Camp. Soon, turn right walking downhill between hedges on Turner's Lane. *Just before the houses you will cross the line of an old Roman road which ran from Badbury Rings in the south to Bath.*

8. At the bottom of the hill are the outskirts of Tarrant Monkton. On arriving at the road, choose right and walk straight ahead past Wyndbrook Cottage and St. Ann's Well. At the ford, cross the Tarrant on the old packbridge continuing ahead, ignoring the road to your right. Return to car. If you want to walk through the ford, beware – it is extremely slippery.

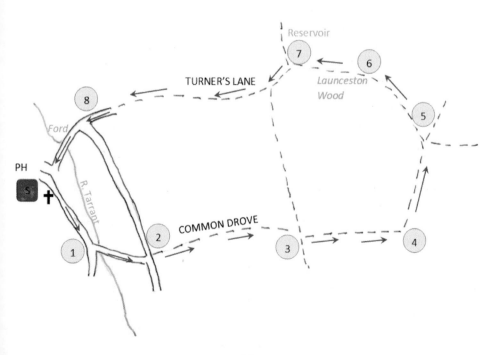

RAMBLE 10 – Around Badbury Rings.

4 miles + 1 mile for wandering in the Rings.

An easy, mainly level route on tracks and grassland. Wonderful views from the Rings and plenty of picnic sites. Possibility of ice-cream van at popular times. Maps: BFCM, 118.

Badbury Rings, part of the Kingston Lacy Estate, and once the site of an Iron Age hillfort of the Durotriges, is arguably the largest and most impressive of such sites in the south of England. There are Palaeolithic and Bronze Age vestiges here but the most substantial settlement was the Iron Age hillfort, a 3-ring construction whose inner ring is thought to date from about 500-600 BCE. When the Roman Second Augusta legion, under the leadership of Vespasian, invaded Britain in AD 43, it was imperative that these hillforts of the Stour valley be occupied to protect the capital of Durnovaria (Dorchester). There have been many archaeological digs in the area and it is clear that following the defeat of the Durotriges, Vespasian established a camp near Lake Farm (now near the A31 in Merley just south of Wimborne) which became the junction of Roman roads to Salisbury, Bath, Dorchester and the port of Poole. The fort itself, 100m above sea level, occupies a site which dominates the countryside all the way to the coast and you can see as far as the Isle of Wight. There are remains of a Romano-Celtic temple to the west and to the south was the town of Vindocladia (near Shapwick), second in size and importance in the area only to Dorchester.

GETTING THERE: Leave Blandford on the B3082 towards Wimborne. About half-way between Blandford and Wimborne there is a sign to the main Badbury Rings car park to the left. It is NT so if a member, scan your card; if not, then pay. There are other smaller car parks which are marked on the map, so you could use these, as they are free, but much smaller. Dogs should be on leads in the Rings themselves and anywhere else where it says so.

After parking the car, walk back downhill to the road.

1. Turn left under the avenue of beech trees. Walk along here for just over a mile, passing one of the smaller car parks at about the half-way stage. *The avenue of beech trees was planted in 1835 by William John Bankes as a birthday present for his mother, Frances. There were, originally, 365 on one side and 366 (for leap-years) on the other, but time and weather (not to mention some negligence pre-1981 before the estate was taken over by the NT) have taken their toll, and there are now many gaps. You will see, however, that re-planting has taken place a little further back from the carriage way.* At the end of the beech tree avenue arrive at the track leading to Lodge Farm. Ignore it and continue along the verge to another very small parking area about 100 yards further on. *Lodge Farm is reputed to have been built as a royal hunting lodge, once the property of John of Gaunt which is held to be the explanation for some of the windows actually being defensive arrow-slits – royals were not very popular in Cranborne Chase at the time of the Peasants' Revolt in 1381.*

2. Take the track to the left, first of all under trees on a wide grassy track; the trees of High Wood are away to the left.

3. At a crossroads (King Down Drove) do not go straight ahead but turn left onto the Drove (also part of the Hardy Way (HW), (a 220-mile long-distance footpath linking places memorable for Hardy and his literary works) following a wide track as it undulates gently, past Highwood Cottage and finally down to a crossroads with fingerpost and a most convenient seat. There is also an information board here regarding the Oaks patch of ancient woodland.

4. Turn right here and walk up past Kingswood Farm (direction Witchampton). *This section of the walk follows the course of the Roman Road (Ackling Dyke) from Poole to Salisbury.*

5. After about ¼ mile, at a stake with signs, leave the HW and turn left onto another track and then down through a wide metal gate. There is no signage on the first side but there is a bridleway sign on the other. Carry on leftwards along this shady track with the Oaks to the left, passing through a hedgeline, still with the wood to the left. At a junction with a

46

wider track, jink left then right across it and carry on in the same direction. Initially, it is quite wide with trees but soon turns narrow with high hedges.

6. At the end of this track arrive at a gate into the Badbury Rings enclosure itself. To regain the car park carry on straight ahead following the fence line or turn left to wander up into Badbury Rings proper. From the top of the Rings can be seen the Kingston Lacy estate, of which the Rings are a part, and on a good day down to Poole harbour. *Kingston Lacy was built for the Bankes family following the destruction of the family home, Corfe Castle, in the English Civil War. It was their home till Ralph Bankes made it over to the NT when he died in 1981. The house itself was in a terrible state of repair and the rest of the estate lacked care as well. However, in spite of the enormous sums needed to renovate it, the NT was persuaded by the spectacular art and antiquaries collection which is unrivalled in a private house.*

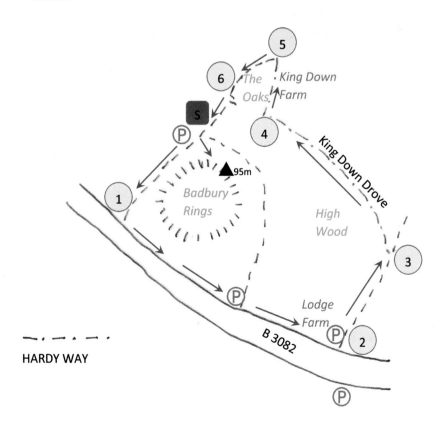

HARDY WAY

RAMBLE 11 – Whitemill and Shapwick

7 to 7 ½ miles

An easy walk largely using the Stour Valley Way (SVW) through fields and on minor roads. Unfortunately, what is arguably the most beautiful section is permanently forbidden to dogs. You can, however, walk along the road to avoid this section. Possibility of refreshment at the Anchor, Shapwick (and ices in the garden at Barford Farm in summer, although not 2021). Maps: BFCM, 118.

Kingston Lacy was built for the Bankes family following the destruction of the family home, Corfe Castle, in the English Civil War and was their home till Ralph Bankes made it over to the NT when he died in 1981. (See Rambles 10 and 12)

GETTING THERE: Leave Blandford on the B3082. At the end of the Beech Tree Avenue take a narrow turning right into a small car park opposite Lodge Farm. If you miss it, you can turn at the entrance to Kingston Lacy and come back.

With the road behind you walk out of the car park along the wide grassy track with the woodland of Kingston Lacy to your left.

1. Ignore all tracks and turnings off to the right until you reach the wooden fingerpost: Stour Valley Way to Sturminster Marshall. Turn right. The route now follows the SVW all the way to Shapwick.
2. Follow the SVW along this track to a lane. Turn right. Just before Barford Farm follow a SVW sign left into a field, now beside the Stour (for herons, swans, coots, moorhens, egrets and kingfishers and other water birds). Keep following the SVW signs through a green corridor, another field and

emerge with Whitemill Bridge to the left and White Mill behind it. *There has been a bridge here since at least the 12th century but this 8-arched Whitemill bridge dates from the 16th century and is part of the Kingston Lacy estate. It is locally famous for the sign on it. The original has, unfortunately been stolen (although there are several others in the county) but a copy has been re-installed.*

Whitecliff Mill was mentioned in the Domesday Book but the current cornmill was built in 1776 and still has its original working parts (renovated 1994). It is unusual in that its machinery is wooden rather than iron and for this reason is too fragile to be in constant use. At the time of its building this would have been an economical choice as wooden parts were cheaper and easier to replace – but you had to do it more frequently!

3. Walk up onto the bridge for a few moments to get a good view up and down the river then return to the road, walking past the Mill; about 100 yards beyond it go left onto NT land, still on the SVW. This is a permissive path and dogs are not allowed on it at any time. In order to continue the circuit with your dog, walk along the road instead into Shapwick. To visit the church, walk down the lane behind the war memorial opposite the Anchor. For the next mile or so the route follows the river. Away to the left, on the other side of the river can be seen the tower of Sturminster Marshall church. There are many stiles and at one point there has been a re-route – don't ignore the NO ENTRY sign. Eventually, leave the fields, arriving at Shapwick via the church. Here leave the SVW.

The beautiful St. Bartholomew's church still has some 12th century Norman features and the tower dates from the 14th century. Just north of Shapwick (Saxon: "sheep village") is the site of the Roman town Vindocladia, second only to Dorchester (Durnovaria) in Wessex in Roman times. Times have changed, however, and now this village's claims to our attention are (in no order of importance): the Anchor for meals, cream teas and general refreshment, its church, the birthplace of Charles Bennett, the first Briton to win an Olympic Gold Medal (1500 metres, 1900) and the home of the Shapwick Monster (actually a crab, see board at the Anchor).

4. Now walk up the High Street, the road beside the Anchor which goes uphill, following the course of a Roman road linking Poole and Badbury Rings.

5. Ignore the first turning on the right (Piccadilly Lane) but take the second one, Park Lane – see a theme here? Gradually ascending, pass New Barn Farm on the right and begin to get glimpses of Badbury Rings up to the left.

6. When the lane ends at a T-junction, carry on straight ahead along a wide track, Sweetbrier Drove.

7. After a couple of hundred yards take a footpath sign to the left through a metal gate. There is a "3" marker to the side. This grassy track goes up, down, then up again and eventually narrows as it makes some sharp turns around some field ends. Finally, the gate leading onto the B3082 is in front of you.

8. Arriving at the main road, turn right and walk along the beech avenue to the end and reclaim car. *(See Ramble 10 for information on beech tree avenue.)*

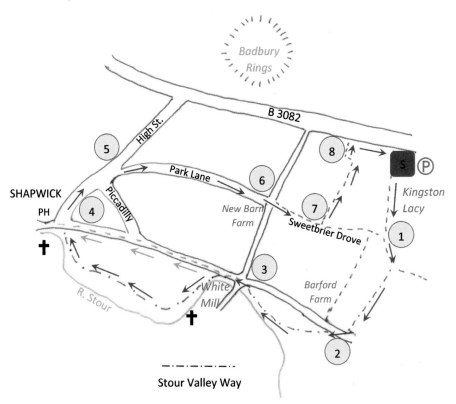

RAMBLE 12 – Pamphill and Kingston Lacy

3 miles

An easy stroll, mostly on paths so good for dogs. Some fairly easy stiles, and two stretches on Stour Valley Way (SVW). Plenty of shade and access to the river approaching Eye Bridge. Some parts can be muddy following wet weather and in the winter. Refreshments possible at Pamphill Dairy and Vine PH. Picnicking in many places, particularly along river. Maps: BFCM, 118.

The entire walk takes place on the National Trust property of Kingston Lacy, their most valuable acquisition ever. Until 1981 it had been in the hands of the Bankes family who had the house built when they were restored to their property after the Restoration of 1660, having had Corfe Castle destroyed and their lands confiscated during the Civil War. The house is small but remarkable, as it is familial rather than palatial, but owing to the enforced exile following a sex scandal of an earlier family member who was a keen art-collector, it has an astonishing collection of pictures and Egyptiana. To visit the house booking is generally essential. Originally built in red-brick it was refaced in Chilmark stone by John Barry in the mid-19th century. Pamphill is a quintessentially estate village with a manor, church, school, cottages and, of course, cricket pitch. St. Stephen's church belongs to the estate, but is of rather more recent vintage, being built in 1907.

GETTING THERE: Leave Blandford on B3082. After the entrance to Kingston Lacy but before Queen Elizabeth's School, take right-hand turn to Pamphill and Pamphill Dairy. Pass the Dairy on the right and when you come to St. Stephen's Church on the right take a left-hand turn into Pamphill Green. There is a car park immediately on the right and also on the left at the other end of the cricket pitch.

From the car park walk back towards the church and just before the T-junction, at the end of the car park, take the track to the left. Turn left onto the lane.

1. After about 50 yards turn down a track on the left, the Stour Valley Way (SVW). This is All Fools' Lane, a sunken path linking the manor of Kingston Lacy to the Court Leet. Passing Candlestick Cottage and evidence of badger setts carry on downhill along a shady track bordered by ferns.

2. At the end of the track come out of the trees. There is a fingerpost for the SVW to the right, but turn left past 1, New Road and then metal gates onto a level, wide grassy track which gradually becomes stony.

3. Emerge at a road at Poplar Farm. Cross the road and take a track to the right of the thatched cottage which has NT signs on it. Follow this track as it becomes shady under the trees. There are two levels here: the higher one next to the field or a lower one which can be muddy. The two versions rejoin at a point where the track takes a left-hand turn. From this point the River Stour is on the right. Continue on this path ignoring any paths off to the side. *The road to Cowgrove which you have just crossed is lined by numerous estate buildings and cottages, including the old Court House where the NT found, on their acquisition of the property, court rolls and scrolls dating back to the 13th century.*

4. Just over a mile from Poplar Farm arrive at Eye Bridge. Walk into the car park and take the SVW signs marked Wimborne ¾ mile into a field/ overflow car park on the right. At the stile, take the route which veers to

the left and walk up to another stile onto the road. Cross the road and then (slightly to the right) take the SVW sign into a field and continue uphill along a grassy track with wild flowers on both sides. Quite soon, cross a stile through the fence to the left, still marked SVW. Staying on the SVW, carry on then go up some forest steps to the left (ignoring the straight on footpath at this junction). Follow this well-trodden SVW uphill.

5. Under an enormous pylon leave the SVW (unless you want to go left to The Vine) going ahead between bushes and then out onto the road just before Pamphill

First School. Turn right onto Pamphill Green again to retrieve car. *Pamphill First School is the only remaining part of a foundation by Ralph Gillingham in 1695 comprising a "Writing School" and Almshouses.*

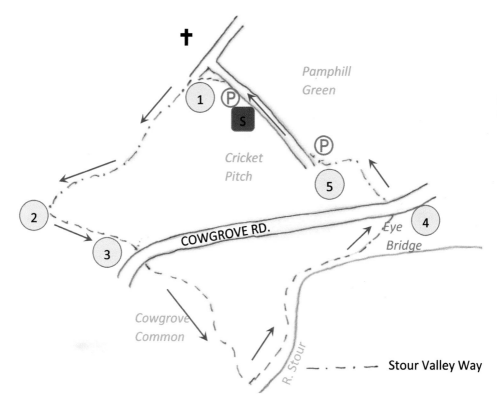

Stour Valley Way

RAMBLE 13 – Spetisbury and Tarrant Crawford

4 miles 3 ¼ miles without Rings

An almost flat walk over easy terrain, although muddy in the winter. Virtually no road walking so good for dogs. Possibility of refreshment at Marcia's Farm Shop or the Scented Botanist at Keyneston Mill (check opening times before departure) and plenty of suitable picnic sites. Maps: BFCM, 118.

GETTING THERE: Leave Blandford heading south towards Poole on the A350. After about 3 miles arrive in Spetisbury. At the far end of the village there is a crossroads; to the right is Louse Lane, but you go left down towards Crawford Bridge. Either park on the left at the end of the houses just before the bridge or further on where the road begins to widen. Alternatively, start from point 7 as there is more formal parking next to the primary school, but it is only available out of school hours. This would give the option of finishing at Marcia's Farm shop and parking there, with permission.

Continue walking along the road, away from the village.

1. After about 400 yards take a footpath sign left into a field, the Stour Valley Way (SVW). *This is a long-distance walking path running from the source of the River Stour at Stourhead to the sea at Christchurch.* Continue along this path around two sides of the same field then follow the path round to the left and through another field, still with the hedge on your left, to emerge onto a metalled road (about ¾ mile).

2. Cross the road and continue through a gate onto a footpath up the side of a field towards a line of telegraph posts and then through a gate following the line of telegraph poles, still following the SVW till arriving at the church. *The church of St. Mary the Virgin is a real little gem. Dating from the 12th century it predates the mighty Crawford Abbey, once the largest Cistercian Nunnery in the country. Its most illustrious inhabitants are Archbishop Poore, who founded Salisbury Cathedral in the early 13th century, and Queen Joan of Scotland, sister to Henry III. Its greatest claim to fame though are its medieval wall paintings depicting the martyrdom of St. Margaret of Antioch, a popular medieval saint.*

3. On leaving the church take the footpath over the Tarrant and continue along beside it for about ¼ mile to a road. *As you walk along this track the lands of Crawford Abbey would have been to your left but little now remains. The Abbey was founded by Ralph de Kahaines in the 12th century (hence Tarrant Keyneston) although it rose to greatness in the time of Archbishop Poore who was born here. There are some medieval barns but the Abbey Farmhouse is somewhat more modern.*

4. Cross the road and almost opposite go through a metal gate onto a footpath (still the SVW) away from the River Tarrant along a track beside a field with the hedge to the left. Not long after passing through a wooden gate are the buildings of Keyneston Mill. *The mill has had many guises in its long history; first as a water-mill, in the 20th century a vineyard and a fruit farm and now it is a perfumed botanic garden with a bistro café and courses for fragrance enthusiasts. This is also where the Tarrant flows into the Stour.*

5. At the end of the track turn left down down past the mill buildings and cross a little bridge onto water meadows. Continuing along this track straight ahead, cross several more bridges as at this point the Stour divides into three as it undulates its way through the meadows. After crossing these meadows carry straight on ahead, still on the SVW and ignoring another footpath from the left.

6. Finally, after a gate, arrive at the Old Mill and its pond, now a private house, and continue over a concrete pedestrian bridge through this wonderful garden and past some old garages until arriving at Marcia's Farm Shop and café at Clapcott's Farm.

7. Cross the main road (A350) and continue straight ahead down West End towards Spetisbury Primary School. Just past the school turn left up a ramp onto the Trailway continuing towards Poole. *This walking and cycling path follows the route of the old Somerset and Dorset railway line which linked Poole to Bath. It was closed down in 1966 and the bridge into Blandford dynamited in the 1970's. It currently runs from Spetisbury through Blandford and for about 11 miles to Sturminster Newton. (The extension to Stalbridge in the north is already under way). There are several information panels along the route, notably at Charlton Halt in the Blandford direction and at the site of the old Spetisbury station which is now looked after by a local railway preservation society.*

After about 300 yards, walk under a bridge. To miss out the Rings, simply continue along the Trailway to Spetisbury Station, as in point 9. **Just before** arriving at Spetisbury station, go down a slope with a handrail on the right onto the lane leading to South Farm. Cross the lane and walk uphill for about 100 yards then take a footpath sign left through an arable field. Ahead is the base of the Rings. Enter through the gap and go right to walk a circuit of the Rings. At the high point is an OS trig point. After wandering at will, leave by the same route to return back across the field to the lane. *Spettisbury Rings (also known as Crawford Castle) is the site of an early Iron Age hillfort, whose bloody history was not known until the major earthworks required for the Somerset and Dorset Railway uncovered a graveyard containing about 100 bodies. They were found to be both Roman legionaries (soldiers of Vespasian's Second Augusta following his invasion of Britain in AD 43) and members of the local tribe, the Durotriges. Spetisbury was one of four hillforts along the Stour which he needed to control in order to set up a local capital at Dorchester.*

8. This time, go back up to the Trailway through the steps on the right rather than the slope on the left and spend a few minutes exploring what was Spetisbury Station. *The Spetisbury Station Project was conceived and worked on by an enthusiastic group of local volunteers (they are always looking for new members!) and is a most atmospheric place to stop and have your picnic as well as look at the renovation.*

In December, Santa always visits to collect his mail!

9. Carry on along the Trailway and at the end of this section turn left down Louse Lane to the crossroads with the A350 and return to car. *Your last view of the River Stour here is one of its most glorious; you cross the river over a medieval pack-bridge and as you look downstream you are likely to be greeted by the sight of egrets or a flotilla of swans. If you wait long enough, there are kingfishers too.*

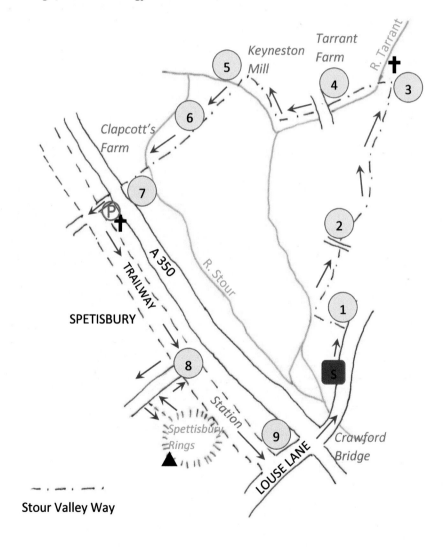

RAMBLE 14 – The Lower Winterbornes

8 miles or 6 miles

A generally flat walk, mainly footpaths and bridleways, very little on road so good for dogs. The route passes through/ by five of the Winterborne villages, including Tomson which has a particularly interesting church and the pretty village of W. Zelston. The bridleways can be muddy in winter and during the winter and spring, the Winterborne is exactly what it says it is (ie a stream which only flows in winter), but in a prolonged dry spell it may be no more than a trickle. Possibility of refreshment at the Greyhound (check opening times) in W. Kingston. Nearby: Botany Inne on A31. Maps: 117.

Its name gives it away; a settlement that once belonged to the Crown and which lies on a small river that runs during the winter. But in 2008 a chance discovery in a field to the north of W.Kingston led to an extensive excavation by archaeologists from Bournemouth University, beginning in 2015. What was uncovered has been described as the first planned settlement in the country. Dating from at least 100BCE (when the other Iron Age settlements in the area, mostly hillforts, were already in decline) was a town of 150-200 roundhouses of which 16 have been examined and many artefacts, bones etc. were found. They named it Duropolis (after the local Celtic tribe, the Durotriges) and it has recast archaeologists' views of ancient life in this area. The earliest part of the walk (past Abbot's Court, previously Turberville Manor) leads us along the line of a Roman road.

GETTING THERE: Leave Blandford on the A354 towards Dorchester and after about 3 miles take a left-hand turn to Winterborne Kingston. Once arrived in the village, take one of the later turns left into Church Lane and park as near as possible to the church. **Behind the church, walk out of town along East Street.**

1. Leaving the village, pass farm buildings on the left and soon arrive at Abbot's Court Retreat. Here, take the diagonally right bridleway sign into the field and continue parallel to the drive (to the Court) with the fence to the left. At the end of the field come out onto a lane and continue along it. *For the shorter route continue straight ahead. Not taking the left-hand turn onto St Edward's Way (SEW) on the main route, continue ahead, still on a bridleway through a field with the hedge to the right. This one may flood at the bottom end in winter, so wellies or give the flood a wide berth. At the end of the field, go through a gap, now walking on a wide grassy path between arable fields. Next, cross a substantial track and then walk through two more fields with gates, still in the same direction. When you exit the last field through a gate, cross the track diagonally left to go through another gate onto the bridleway, walking gently uphill on a protected path with trees and bushes to both sides. Finally, at a junction with bridleway signs, turn right into a field and continue from *** [5].*

2. When the track takes a left-hand turn follow it; this is now St. Edward's Way (SEW) (even if there are no signs). When the farm track peters out at a barn, continue on the narrow bridleway to the left of the barn, between hedges. Where the protected path ends, emerge into a field and continue left, walking with hedge to left, the track is quite clear. These routes continue to the end of the field, then jink right for about 150 yards and then left, still on SEW, now walking at the side of a field, hedge to the right.

3. At the end of field there is a metal gate. Do not go through it, but take the narrow bridleway to the right, Little Coll Wood. At this point the route leaves SEW. In less than 100 yards, follow a bridleway right, through the trees (no signage, but there is a distinct route) crossing a wider track. *If you miss it, continue to end of wood and follow edge round to the right and then, after a couple of hundred yards, take a broad grassy path/ bridleway on the right, then pick up the bridleway to the left – follow the hooves!*

4. At the end of the wood, exit into a field, following the signs right and then left along two sides of the open field until arriving at the trees of Great Coll Wood. Follow the bridleway signs right, through a gate, initially beside the wood but fairly soon through a gate and into the wood itself still on the bridleway.

5. ***At the end of the wood, there is a junction of routes; take the footpath towards the left signed through a farm-gate into a grassy field. Walk down hill, keeping to the left-hand boundary and then right, along the bottom edge of the field as far as a gap. Pass through this onto the track and then road past Bushes Farm. Continue for about ½ a mile gently up and down to W. Zelston. As you breast the rise you can see the Charborough Tower away to the left. *The beautiful little village of W. Zelston (name probably derives from Zeals/ de Seles family) has deservedly won many awards as Best Kept Village in Dorset and its situation on the Winterborne stream only adds to its attraction. In just a few steps you can visit it before continuing on your way. There is a very informative board by the river and to visit the Botany Bay Inne take the first left out of the village and up to the A31.* To visit the village, continue ahead, towards the church and river. Then return, taking the left-hand turn to the Village Hall.

6. The route now turns right just before the church, a footpath marked 2¼ miles to W. Kingston and the Village Hall. Follow the footpath signs through two fields to a gate into Riverside Farm. Follow the footpath signs; after a few yards, up to the right and then left out onto a metalled road lined with trees.

7. At the end of this road turn left into W. Tomson to visit the Norman church and then return to this point. *St. Andrew's church in (Winterborne) Tomson is one of only four single-cell Norman churches still extant in the country.*

Its structure may be 12th century, but the wooden roofing is late medieval and the box-pews (graded in size from back to front according to social status) were given by local worthy Archbishop William Wake in the 18th century. By Victorian times, however, it was used only by farm animals and would probably have fallen down had it not been rescued by the Society for the Preservation of Ancient Buildings, who were fortunate enough to own some Thomas Hardy manuscripts which they sold for £1,000 to finance its restoration in tribute to the great writer who, having worked here as a

young architect, was known to treasure this little church. Tomson Farmhouse, nearby, is a Jacobean manor house. Now go left (or right if you've not visited the church) through a gate into a grassy field and cross it following the footpath arrow direction.

Go through another metal gate into a field and carry on keeping the hedge to your left. Cross a small plank bridge over a stream and then continue on path behind Anderson Manor. *This manor appears in the Domesday Book and in medieval times was held by the Turberville family (of Bere Regis). It was sold to the Mortons in the 15th century who started to build the present manor in 1613, selling it to the Tregonwells of Milton Abbas who completed it in 1622. Constructed of brick (very modern in this period) and stone it is considered to be one of the finest examples of a small Jacobean manor house in the country. It had a church, St. Andrew's, which is now redundant and used as a private chapel. By the early 20th century it was seriously dilapidated but had a new lease of life during WW2 when it was taken over by the Ministry of War and used as a training base with obstacle course and firing range, initially by 62 Commando and subsequently, SOE. After the war, parcels of land were sold off and it is now a private family home.*

8. Cross a bridleway on the footpath sign through an arable field, skirting farm buildings to the left and down to a 5-bar gate. Go through gate and turn right along fence line over a tiny stream. About half-way along this field there is a footpath sign to the right; ignore it. At the end of this field pass through a gate and out into an arable field. Look at the short row of trees ahead and aim for the right-hand edge of them and then on through another gate into another field following footpath direction. Path then bends round a house on the left, then through a gate and out onto a lane; turn right. Arriving at the farm buildings jink right and then almost immediately left through a gateway by a brick and wood single-storey building into a grassy field, following arrows, hedge to the left. Follow this path round and out onto the lane at Abbot's Court Dairy, then left and back to car.

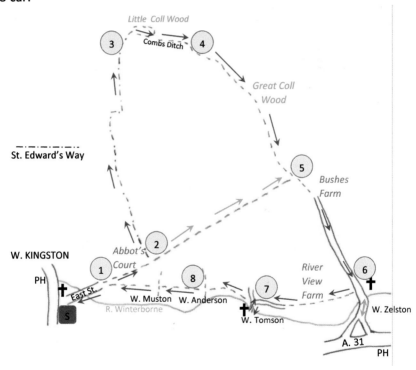

Ramble 15 – Milton Abbas, Winterbornes Stickland and Glenston

7 ½ miles or 6 miles

This is an interesting woodland walk, with lots of opportunities for dogs. The longer version has the advantage of exploring the pretty village of W. Stickland, but the shorter route has less road. The circuits both start and finish on the Jubilee Trail. Neither are flat, but there are no particularly long or steep ascents or descents. Refreshment opportunities are the Crown in W. Stickland and the Hambro Arms or the Clipper Tea Room in Milton Abbas. Maps: BFCM, Explorer 117.

The main street of Milton Abbas is frequently featured on calendars of English villages. The estate of Milton Abbey was acquired by the Tregonwell family (the founders of Bournemouth) following the Dissolution of the Monasteries and having been largely used as a farm changed hands in the mid 18th century. The new owners, the Damers, were keen to tidy up the somewhat dilapidated abbey buildings surrounded by labourers' cottages and set about emulating the new owner of Crichel House (see Ramble 7). So in order for the Damers to feel at home in their estates, Capability Brown was engaged to design the gardens and parkland, a Gothic style house was commissioned from Sir William Chambers and finished off by Thomas Wyatt, and the villagers' cottages were demolished. The new village was built for them, but as it is in a steep-sided valley it was extremely inconvenient for people who were expected to grow much of their own food. The estate was later owned by the Hambro family who saved the church from falling down and the abbey has been Milton Abbey School since 1954. If you wish to see the abbey, walk down the village street, take the right-hand fork to Hilton and after about 100 yards take the footpath

off to the left just before the thatched cottage. A stroll of about ¾ mile takes you past the lake and to the door of the abbey.

GETTING THERE: Leave Blandford on the A354 towards Dorchester. In Winterborne Whitechurch, take the second right-hand turn to Milton Abbas and after a couple of miles take the left-hand turn to Milton Abbey, then park in the main street near the Hambro Arms. **Walk back up the hill and just after the village picnic site on the left, take the Jubilee Trail (JT) marker (which you will be following all the way to W. Stickland) off to the left towards Haydon Plantation. Follow the track round past the houses and then turn right out onto the road, towards the telephone box.**

1. Cross the road, walking along a metalled lane, past Milton Manor into Milton Park Wood; first downhill, then just after a big yellow archway, turn left uphill. After descending, jink left then right to follow the JT uphill, and arriving at a junction with a wider track, turn right onto it. Follow all signs for JT, there are several tracks off to both sides, but keep following JT and eventually, after about a mile, go down a dip, then up the other side and come to a fork.

2. For the shorter route, take the right fork (bridleway). As the trees end, walk down the side of a field with the hedge to the left. Follow this track downhill then out onto a road. Turn right down the road for about 500 yards as far as Clenston Manor (on the left). Re-join main route at point 5. Here the JT goes left (longer route). After leaving the trees of Charity Wood, turn right along the side of a field and after about 50 yards turn left across the field to a metal gate. Go straight through the gate, carrying on straight ahead (ignore bridleway sign) and follow the left-hand hedge downhill. At the bottom of the field pass into the next field (grassy) and go diagonally right across it to come to a wide gate about half-way along the top of the field. Pass through the gate and past Valley View Farm out onto Dunbury Lane.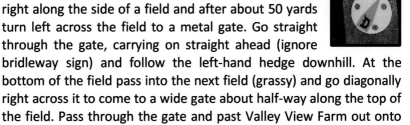

3. Being careful of the traffic (it tends to be a bit fast here) jink right and then left through a gate to descend behind houses into W. Stickland. Here, turn right down the road to the village centre, leaving the JT. *Stickland is a substantial village – even at the time of the Domesday Book (1086) it was a very rich possession, part of the later Milton Abbey*

Estate. The centre of the village is the Cross Tree – a lime which is about 300 years old and beside which you can see the remains of a medieval preaching cross dating from the 15ᵗʰ century. There are references to these (and many other aspects of the village) on the Village Sign on a piece of grass near the school. This sign was created by local craftsmen and unveiled by the sculptress and local celebrity Dame Elizabeth Frink (see Ramble 17) in 1988. It was renovated in 2017, featuring on BBC's "Repair Shop". The last "owners" of Stickland were the banking Hambro family who presented the village with its hall in 1934, but as their fortunes diminished the estate was sold off by auction in 1939.

4. For a small village, there are a lot of roads in W. Stickland. Walk out of the village on the road to W. Whitechurch for about a mile. *On your right you will soon see Quarleston Farm, the oldest house in the village, (and one of the oldest manors in the*  *county) whose central hall with its beautiful timbered roof dates back to the 15ᵗʰ century and since its restoration 30 years ago, now two dwellings. On the opposite side, further on, lies Clenston Manor. It too dates back to the late 15ᵗʰ century (built by a nobleman who was astute enough to choose Henry Tudor in 1485). Slightly further on (on the right) is its Tithe Barn; both are grade 1 listed buildings dating from Tudor times. The Manor has remained in the hands of the same family since about 1230 (though the name has frequently changed) but since one of their other properties is preferred as a family home the Manor has been tenanted for most of its eight centuries.*

5. Opposite Clenston Manor, take a bridleway uphill marked to the Cottage in the Woods. Just after Clenston Lodge (the Cottage) on the right, veer left past an old gateway. There are many cross tracks but ignore them all and go straight ahead. Approaching the end of Oatclose Wood the track turns slightly to the right so that you are walking almost along the side of a field. Arriving at a gate with a footpath sign, follow it steeply downhill, walking with the wood to the right and the grassy field to the left.

6. At the bottom, turn left along the track, now with field to left and Whatcombe Wood to right. At the end of the field there is a junction of tracks; turn right, Whatcombe Common to right and Cliffe Wood up to left. Continue along this track as far as a fork. Go left, there is a grassy field in front of you, but do not enter it; continue left uphill, and then up into a field with a hedge to the left. At the top of the field, ignore the footpath marker ahead but turn right along the hedge-line (walking with hedge to the left), coming out on to the road at Luccombe Riding Centre.
7. Cross road and carry straight on up lane. At top of hill is a junction to re-join JT. The sign is old, but it's there. Turn right here onto JT, trees to the left, hedge to the right, then at entrance to field continue straight ahead along the side of field with hedge to the right. After several hundred yards, there is a signpost on the right in the trees. Take the Milton Abbas ¼ mile direction, across arable field, making for a metal gate in the fence diagonally left. Pass through this gate, over track, then through an old wooden one. Follow JT signs down through the trees to the road. Then walk down hill to car.

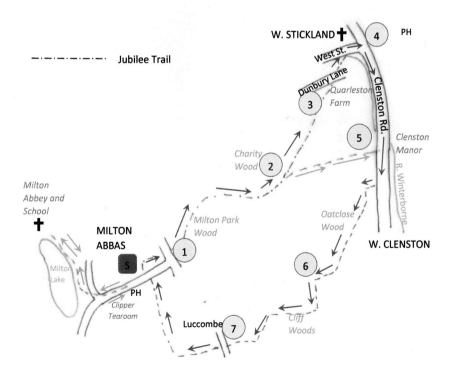

67

RAMBLE 16 – Ansty, the Melcombes and the Dorset Gap

8 miles or 5 ⅓ miles

Not a flat walk, but the ascents and descents are neither long nor too steep, so accessible for most people. It passes two beautiful Tudor manor houses, two lost medieval villages and the Dorsetshire Gap with marvellous views. Much of the walk is on tracks and where there are lanes they are mainly quiet so good for dogs. The walk consists of 2 loops, 1-6 and 7-9, which can be done separately. To do the first loop only, when you get to 6, just carry on after walking back through the village of Melcombe Bingham to re-gain the Village Hall in Ansty. To do the second loop only, walk down the hill across the bridge and turn left onto a footpath*** just after the bridge and follow instructions from point 7. Possibility of refreshment is the Fox Inn at Ansty near beginning/ end of walk. Maps: Explorer 117.

The recent history of Ansty is the history of the Hall and Woodhouse Brewery, founded here by Charles Hall in 1777. The original brewery is now Ansty Village Hall (a new brewery was built in Blandford in 1900) which explains the stream at the bottom of the hill being called the Mash Water. A later partner, Edward Woodhouse, married into the Hall family and thus began the Hall and

Woodhouse story. The Fox Inn was originally a Hall family home and the family still own other properties in the parish, including Higher Melcombe House.

GETTING THERE: Leave Blandford on the A354 west towards Dorchester. After about 6 miles, turn right in Milborne St. Andrew (signed to Hilton) and after 1½ miles turn left to Ansty Cross. After several miles, follow the brown signs to the Fox Inn. As you pass the Fox on your left, going downhill, continue a bit further down, parking on the right at the Village Hall (VH). **With VH behind you, walk right, downhill and over bridge and up other side to walk into Melcombe Bingham, pausing only to note the footpath going off to the left at the far side of the bridge, by the sign with "Jubilee 2013" (as well as NO PARKING) as you will be returning to this. (Point 7)**

1. Just after the village sign, at the beginning of the houses, take a (green) sign right to Melcombe Park Farm; this is Cothayes Drove. Walk up here for about a mile to Cothayes House and Farm and as metalled path veers rightish slightly uphill follow it, ignoring all other paths, to walk beside Breach Wood on your right.
2. At the end of the wood where the path takes a sharp left turn (by Dorset Eco Retreats) follow it to join the Wessex Ridgeway (WR) (a walking and riding long-distance route which crosses Dorset from Ashmore to Lyme Regis). At Melcombe Park Farm jink right and then left through the farmyard and at end of farm buildings there are 3 options; take the furthest right, signed Dorsetshire Gap, which goes through a gate and diagonally right across a field. Do not be fooled by the tractor tracks going straight up, but follow the direction favouring the bottom (right), a slight path, rather than the top of the field to make for a double gate on the far side. Pass through it and then follow a very vague path diagonally right up

to the crest of the ridge. Then turn right to walk along the ridge, the path is fairly clear. There are spectacular views here and you can see the steep sides of Nettlecombe Tout, an Iron Age hill fort in the distance in front of you. Eventually, the path leads downhill out through a gate to a junction of tracks. This is the Dorsetshire Gap, and it's a tradition to sign the book (see below).

The Dorsetshire Gap has been a major junction of five routes from medieval times to the nineteenth century, accessible only on foot. The Wessex Ridgeway

(part of the ancient trading route from Norfolk to Devon) passes through here and is situated at a gap between steep hills which separates the chalk valleys in the east from the Blackmore Vale. The steep slopes to the west of the Gap are Nettlecomb Tout, an Iron Age hill fort. It has a timeless and romantic quality to it and all visitors are invited to sign (and put a comment in) the visitors' book which resides in a weatherproof box kept under a tree at the side of the pass.

3. From this junction of ways, take the WR route marked to Folly, which goes gradually uphill through trees. On exiting the trees, go through a gate in the fence line up into a grassy field, following the WR direction (Folly 1). The track leads almost exactly to a gate in the top right-hand corner of the field. Go through it, still following the WR direction ahead. At the top of the field, there is a small concrete and brick construction.

4. At this point, leave the WR turning left, following a bridleway through two fields with the hedge to the left. There are ancient cross dykes here, trees to the left. When the trees end there is a junction of routes.

5. Turn left, going through 2 gates, signed Higher Melcombe ½ mile. Then

follow a wide tractor track curving downhill towards farm. At the bottom, go through a small gate on right (not farmyard) and walk along the side of a field. Then out through another gate, left for about 50 yards and out onto a lane, turning right, walking past medieval Melcombe Horsey and Higher Melcombe Manor and Chapel. After the manor, rejoin metalled lane with line of beech trees, past the pump house and onto the houses at Cross Lanes.

The medieval village of Melcombe Horsey, visible now only by lumps and bumps in the field to the left by the farm, is one of two LMVs (Lost Medieval Villages) on this route. Both were no doubt affected by the Black Death and were effectively extinct by the beginning of the 15th century. The L-shaped Tudor Manor House here is unusual as it has an integral chapel, whose stained-glass window you will see as you walk past. The Horseys acquired it in the 16th century but following some unwise speculation in coal-mining it was bought by the Frekes in 1588 who rebuilt the chapel and turned it into one of the greatest houses in Dorset. From 1707 to 1919 it belonged to the Pitt Rivers Estate. During this time it was tenanted and much of the house was pulled down to provide stone for the Ansty Brewery. It was finally bought by the Woodhouse family just before WW2, who have commissioned new commemorative windows (to John and Elizabeth Horsey and also the Woodhouse botanist Charles, who bought it in 1938).

6. At a junction is a bus-shelter and telephone box. Turn left here and walk back into and through the village of Melcombe Bingham.

7. After leaving the houses and descending the hill, take the footpath*** (previously noted) on the right, through a gate, walking with Devil's Brook to the left. Follow the direction of the footpath signs through two more wooden gates and out into a grassy field, still going in same direction with fence to left (may be very muddy in winter). On arriving at a little wooden bridge cross it. After the bridge, take the path to the left, going uphill, soon walking along the left-hand side of an arable field on a cliff high above the Devil's Brook. Reaching the corner of the field, go through another wooden gate, now walking through trees. Ignore the wooden bridge which soon appears on the left. As the trees end, enter the estate of Bingham's Melcombe.

The first Bingham came here in the early 13th century when he married a Turberville heiress, and over the next few centuries their descendants gradually acquired more land for the manor. The manor you see here now was built in the mid 16th century when the formal gardens were laid out too. It is thought to be one of the best examples of a Tudor courtyard manor in the country. There were additions and changes in the next two centuries but it remained pretty much the same until 1895 when it was finally sold out of the family and bought by a keen naturalist, Reginald Bosworth-Smith, who was a teacher at Harrow. A later owner, Lord Southborough, in the mid 20th century modernised a mansion which had only one toilet, no electricity or bathrooms and was lit by oil lamps. He also commissioned Geoffrey Jellicoe and Brenda Colvin to restore the gardens. In 1980 the estate was acquired by John Langham (of Langham Industries, a major UK engineering group) and subsequently his son developed his father's small vineyard into the large-scale enterprise it is now. There has been a church on this site since 1150, but the current St. Andrew's dates from the 14th century. It was a Bingham family church for centuries and there are many memorials to famous Binghams. (One was a leading Colonel on the Parliamentary side in the Civil War when BM was the regional HQ for their army.) The open land to the east of the church is the site of the other lost medieval village of our walk. The manor is now a private house, but the church may be visited.

8. This is private land so keep to the permissive paths. Go right, along the grassy promenade, past the beautiful and ancient yew hedge, and then left along the gravel track to pass the house. Ignore the drive coming in from the right and walk to the left of the church. Crossing the Devil's Brook over a little black metal bridge, take the right-hand option over a small field to a stile out onto a lane. Turn left up the lane and after a few hundred yards, when it turns left, continue straight on ahead, now on a wide chalky track between hedges. Soon start to climb through trees.

9. Just before the top, there is a junction with a cross track. Turn left onto a wide grassy path downhill marked "No horses". There is a footpath off to the left about half-way down, ignore it. At the end of the grassy track turn left along a bridleway (no signage) down the sides of two fields and then exit out onto a lane between Rose and Ivy Cottages. Go right, through the hamlet of Aller and at the end of Aller Lane arrive back at the Village Hall (or turn right for the Fox).

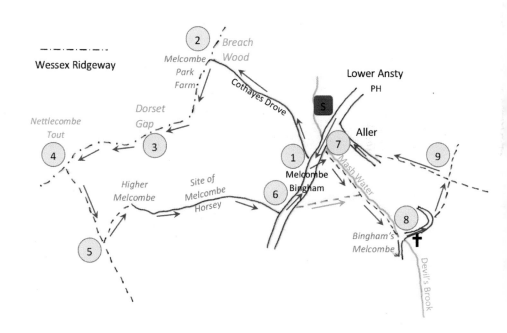

RAMBLE 17 Ibberton

13 miles (or 7 ½ miles or 5 ½ miles)

A challenging walk as this part of Dorset is very hilly, but the pay-off resides in the wonderful views which are to be had on a clear day and the discovery of out-of-the-way villages. It is also quite difficult to find your way around the myriad of country lanes. Ensure that you read this description before you set off! It is composed of two loops, but either can be done independently. The first loop is undulating, but the second has a steep ascent and descent. An OS map or similar is very useful for this walk, as is a compass.There are plenty of suitable picnic spots, notably, Ringmoor, Bonsley Common and Rawlsbury Camp. There is also the Ibberton PH in the village, which lies on the second loop (check opening times). At Baker's Folly, Tiny Tim's offers ice-creams and drinks/refreshments at weekends and Bank Holidays in season (from Good Friday), as well as most days in summer holidays.

GETTING THERE: From Blandford, take the A350 north, turning onto the A357 in Durweston, a mile or so from Blandford. In Shillingstone, take a left-hand turn to Okeford Fitzpaine and in the village take a left towards Ibberton and then Bulbarrow/ Woolland. Arriving at Belchawell Street (the Cross) go left towards Bulbarrow until you come to Ibberton Hill car park.

(Alternatively, take the W. Stickland road (NW) out of Blandford, then from Stickland take the sign to W. Houghton. At the telephone box in the village, turn right up the narrow road to Bulbarrow. On arriving at a junction where several roads merge with each other, turn extremely sharp right past the large Woolland Hill parking area (unsigned) which has the panoramic view over Bulbarrow. After about a mile, Ibberton Hill car park is on your right.)

If you are planning on doing only the first loop (1 - 8) then the car park and picnic spot on Okeford Hill is probably more convenient; in which case, from BF take Fairmile Road west to to W. Stickland, then take a right turn to Turnworth and after you have passed through the village park in the Okeford Hill car park and begin the circuit from (2). To do the second loop only, there is easier parking at Bulbarrow (marked as Woolland Hill on OS) and then begin at point (15) continuing from (8) at Ibberton Hill car park.

The first part of the walk is on the Wessex Ridgeway. Facing out towards the road, leave the car park by walking right, downhill, on a grassy track following the WR. On arriving at the road, continue walking in the same direction past Baker's Folly.

1. After about ½ mile, where road continues ahead, take a track gently uphill on the right, signposted Okeford Hill (WR) 1 ¾ miles. Pass transmitter mast. Path narrows, carry on straight ahead still on WR, avoiding left fork. Arrive at right-hand track (NT) off onto Ringmoor and Turnworth Down (info board). Explore Ringmoor Down and then retrace steps or continue along WR. *Ringmoor and Turnworth Down is now owned and managed by the NT. It is an extremely extensive site of a Celtic-Romano settlement and one of Dorset's Iron Age hillforts. The bumps in the ground testify to the village that once sprawled across this down. Latterly, it has been used as pastureland by local people but there were cottages here until the 1950's when they were demolished; there are, however, still a few vestiges remaining on the right, not long after entering the enclosure.*

2. At Okeford Hill car park and picnic site, cross the road and continue on the WR ahead. (But before doing so, it is worth walking a few yards up the road to the left to the Okeford Beacon with its spectacular views.) After about ¼ mile, there is a

sharp left, but carry on ahead on WR past a wide gate. Walking across the top here, with trees to the left, look out for a trig point ahead and away to the right.

3. Make for this, leaving the WR and continue walking on a grassy path signed to Bonsley Common. After several hundred yards turn right onto a grassy path, no signage) which goes slightly downhill between arable fields to the corner of Bonsley Wood and the remains of a dewpond. Arriving at the corner of the wood, continue to follow the bridleway along the side of it. At the end of the first side, turn left along the second side now following the St. Edward's Way.

4. At the end of the trees, continue ahead, now along a track with a field to the left and a hedge/ trees to the right. At the end of this field, arrive at a junction, Jubilee Trail left and straight on. Turn right here, following a track downhill to a road.

5. Turn right uphill, walking through the tiny village of Turnworth. *As you walk through the village, the house names will betray earlier usage. It is tiny, but attractive, and the ancient tree, near the post-box and telephone kiosk still has a use as a notice-board. The parish church of St. Mary dates from medieval times, but only the tower is original, most being the result of Victorian renovation (architect assisted by the young Thomas Hardy). It used to boast a substantial Jacobean Manor House, but it was burnt down in the 1940's.*

6. Arriving in the village, take the first bridleway to the left (after Jasmine Cottage), uphill, and at the top, at a junction of routes, turn left, along the side of a field, hedge to the left. Continue along the second side of the field and then follow the track for about 50 yards and go through a gateway, descending down through a grassy field, fence to the left and then out onto a wide chalky track.

7. Turn right up this track, behind you are the lambing sheds at Pleck. Ignore a bridleway off to the left and also another track. At the junction of bridleways, leave this chalky path, taking a bridleway left-ish up the left-hand side of a field. At the top of the incline, follow the signs, now with some trees to the left. At the end of the trees, follow bridleway sign, straight ahead over stony field. At end of second stand of trees, there are no signs, but keep on ahead, slightly uphill across the field to a gate. Go through the gate onto an enclosed track and follow it back to IH car park.

8. Cross road and go through gate onto hillside. The OS map shows a left then right zigzag, but it is easier to walk right, along the top of the field, then follow the treeline downhill until almost at the bottom of the trees there is a gap. Turn right through the gap, then bear left downhill and after about 50 yards, at a telegraph pole, go through a gap and walk right so that the hedge is to the right. Continue along the field-line, making some

adjustments to follow the bridleway (follow the hooves), eventually walking between fences, along to a gate and out onto a lane. Cross the road and continue on this Halter Path to Ibberton. The path swings left and steeply down hill, passing the church on the left and then down between houses (and the Ibberton PH on the left) to a T-junction. *Ibberton was, until the 1970's, owned by the Rivers family. Its church is unusual in several different ways; it is one of only three in the country to recognise the Roman saint Eustachius, it is still largely 15th century (Victorian restoration was minimal and sensitively carried out) and it occupies an unusual position, high on the hill, necessitating a climb for the villagers – fortunately the pub, the Ibberton, which has stood on this site since Tudor times, still remains. It nestles under the cliff hillside of Bulbarrow, tucked away from the rest of the world.*

9. Here go left, taking the lane signed to Woolland. Follow it as it turns left past Cross Farm. Where the lane turns right, at a sign left to Bulbarrow, leave the road and carry on straight ahead into a grassy area, walking with the fence to your left, following the footpath direction. Walk with the fence to the left for a few hundred yards slightly downhill and then through a metal gate over a wooden bridge to a protected pathway. It can be very muddy here where narrow, even in dry weather. At the end of this path, go over a stile into a field. Follow direction of footpath arrow towards a telegraph pole, then cross the drive to Chitcombe Farm. Continue in same direction towards another telegraph pole (and sign to the farm) and on arriving at the hedge, walk about 15 yards to the right to find a hidden gap

which leads down to a little bridge. Then follow the footpath signs through several small fields to finally exit out through a metal kissing-gate and out onto the road. *Woolland was originally a chapelry held by Milton Abbey but was secularised at the Dissolution. There have been a whole succession of Manor Houses here since the 16th century, but the current one is a refurbishment and extension of the stables of the 1731 house, which was mostly demolished in 1772. In its current identity it was, in the 1970s the last home of the sculptress Dame Elizabeth Frink. (An older house, probably Tudor in origin, went through many travails before being comprehensively renovated in the late 20th century and renamed The Parsonage). There has been a parish church here since the 14th century, but the current one is Victorian, designed by Sir Gilbert Scott (Houses of Parliament). Its church boasts an ancient yew tree more than 2,000 years old.*

10. Now walk left, through the village, passing Woolland House, Manor House and church. Where the lane swings left, by another Woolland sign, keep ahead onto a footpath. At last habitation on left (at end of gravel), take a footpath right through a kissing-gate ignoring footpath right onto a grassy track between trees. At the end, go through a kissing gate, ignoring footpath right and walk ahead along side of field, hedge to the right (can be very wet here). Then through kissing-gate in corner of field and up through a small strip of trees, then another field, up and down over the grass keeping to the right.

11. Do not follow pathway down to the gate at the bottom of the field, but just before the end, take a footpath sign right through a gate, which leads down through trees and over a little bridge, then up past Stoke Wake church where you turn right onto a driveway and then left up a drive to the road. Out on the road, turn left uphill, past the barns and stables. *The village of Stoke Wake has a long history, being recorded in the Domesday Book, but it lost its parish status several years ago and is now attached to*

Hazelbury Bryan. Its Victorian church is also redundant, being now in private hands. The Old Rectory which you can see down to the left is now a stud farm, so the statue in the grounds is not a surprise.

12. After 200-300 yards, find signs on the right to a footpath(right) and a bridleway (left). Take the bridleway. At the end of the trees, go through a gate into a grassy field going uphill, walking next to the right-hand fence. Not long after you start to go downhill the path swings left, facing you is a chalky cliff. The track leads to a metal gate, go through it. Walk along the top side of the field, then the second side. Just before a gap between hedges turn left to go through a gap in the trees up a path to a gate. Go through it and continue uphill, fence to the right.

13. After about 50 yards, ignore the WR signs right through a gate to the right, but a few yards futher on, also on the right, follow the direction of a fingerpost in the trees marked ¾ mile to Bulbarrow. It goes left and straight uphill to another gate, pass through it and carry on up to Rawlsbury Camp.

Follow the path round the right-hand side of the fort, then pass through another gate. When the track forks, do not go right (downhill) but keep to the left track towards a gate. This ends at a metal gate (still WR) out onto the road.

14. Continue on WR right and up road. Once on the road, ignore a left turn (Woolland) and a right fork (Ansty), but don't forget to turn and look back over the camp stretching away below. *Rawlsbury Camp is the largest Iron Age hillfort in Dorset and is, arguably, the most scenic. As you walk back*

up the road after leaving the fort, make sure to stop and look back at the magnificent views from Bulbarrow out over the fort. It was used as a beacon at the time of the fear of the Spanish Armada in 1588 and also as a telegraph point station during the Napoleonic wars. The simple but imposing wooden cross was erected in 1966 by the Mid-Dorset Common life Council of Churches, an ecumenical Christian initiative supported by over 20 parishes. Its first gathering in July 1967 was marred by dreadful weather, but nonetheless, was attended by over 3,000 parishioners with another 1,000 having to be turned away for lack of space. The services continued through the 60s and into the 70s.

15. After just over a mile come to a junction. Go left and left again to arrive at a large car park on the right. (Woolland Hill, but currently un-marked). Continue along this road for about a mile to return to IH car park (last few hundred yards you can walk up on the grass to the right.)

Bulbarrow Hill is the highest point in Dorset, which explains both the steep climbs and the wonderful views. It also explains the transmitter masts which lie to your right as you climb back up the hill.

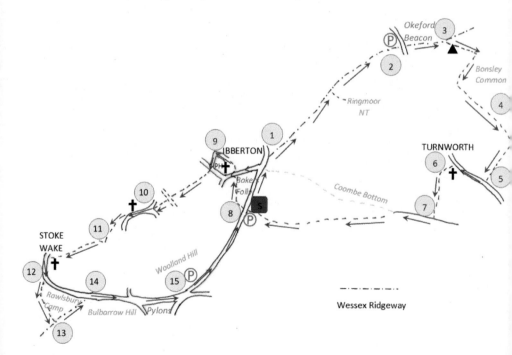

RAMBLE 18 – Durweston, Stourpaine, and Hod Hill

4 ½ miles

A fairly easy walk with one major ascent. Refreshment is to be had at the White Horse in Stourpaine (only 100 yards off your route) or alternatively, have a picnic high up on Hod Hill with its wonderful views over the Stour valley. Cattle may be grazing in the enclosure of Hod Hill itself, so you have two options; to walk through them or to take the path around the perimeter, point 4. Maps: BFCM (portion), 118 (portion)

GETTING THERE: Leave Blandford on the A350 going north. After about a mile, turn left onto the A357 towards Sturminster Newton. In about ½ mile, take a left-hand turn into Durweston. Very soon, turn left again towards the school and village hall. Park just after the school. *Walk a bit further along the road as far as the recreation field, then look back and you will see the reclaimed sign-board for Durweston and Stourpaine Halt. This station on the Somerset and Dorset line was opened in 1928 but the line was closed during the Beeching cuts of 1966. The actual site of the station is elsewhere. Durweston and Stourpaine are twin settlements, being situated on either bank of the Stour.*

Durweston was a thriving village on the Portman Estate in earlier times, but the demise of the railway and the pre-eminence of the car led to its losing its many local businesses by the 1980's. However, the village is growing again now, the school is thriving and a new Village Hall points to a lively community atmosphere. There has been a village here since well before the Domesday Book which listed it as having three vineyards. The church predates 1381, but although there are medieval features it was largely re-built by the Portmans in the mid 19th century. **Walk back up the road to the T-junction with Milton Road. Go right here, back to the A357, cross the road and walk left for about 100 yards to take a bridleway which is a wide stony track on the right.**

1. First, walk between two fields, then past the old mill. Follow the track round to the left and then the right, then cross an old metal bridge over another arm of the Stour and under the old railway bridge which now bears the North Dorset  Trailway. *At this point you are as close as you are going to get to the site of the old station.* Just after the bridge, take a narrow path on the left between fields marked as the White Hart Link. (This is the shortest route here, but if you prefer to walk on a wider path, you can continue ahead for a few yards to take the North Dorset Trailway instead.) Soon arrive at Stourpaine church. *By the 19th century the villagers of both Stourpaine and Durweston were living in conditions of great poverty, partly caused by the Corn Laws, and all dwellings were owned by the Portman Estate. The Poor Law Commission commented particularly on the wretched state of the peasantry of Dorset but things are very different now, the village of Stourpaine having a well-kempt and prosperous look to it, a lively community shop within the public house (The White Horse) and a certain notoriety as being the last resting place of the Duchess of Cornwall's father who spent his latter years living with his other daughter here in the village.*

2. Carry on straight ahead through the village. In about 100 yards, take a left-hand turn, Havelins, signed to the village hall and playing field.

3. At the end of the lane (entrance to the Trailway towards Sturminster Newton) turn right into Hod Drive. Walk up a wide track with Hod Hill ahead. Eventually, the track veers to the right and goes slightly downhill, now under trees with the River Stour on the left. In some places the track has a choice of two levels but they both join up again. Gradually, the path rises above the river veering right under trees as the river goes off to the left.

4. After about ½ mile arrive at a woodland car park and go right, uphill, through a gate, up onto Hod Hill. The track uphill is clearly marked, straying only a few yards from the fence to your right. *Hod Hill is the largest of the Iron Age hillforts occupied by Roman forces under Vespasian following his victory over the Britons at the battle of Medway in 43 A.D. The legionaries of the Second Augusta needed to occupy the four Stour Valley forts in order to establish a capital at Dorchester and protect it from attack by the locals. Many artefacts dating from this period have been found here as well as the vestiges of about 50 roundhouses from the Celts who were defeated by the superior Roman troops.* At a second gate, the entrance to the site of the fort, there is a sign about a bull in the field. The alternative here is the circuitous route; go left and walk around a sector of the enclosure then come to a gate marked as a bridle way. Go through here, and then another

gate, to walk along the edge of a field. At the end of the field, follow it round and then within about 100 yards leave the field through a metal gate out onto a track. This track uphill takes you straight into the enclosure but you turn left and walk downhill to point 5. **Otherwise, go through the second gate. The hillfort is roughly square. Entry is at the NW corner; to cross it, proceed along a diagonal, direction SE, to the opposite corner and exit out onto a track going downhill.** *Having been untouched by modern farming, this chalk grassland is a haven for butterflies and wild flowers including orchids in the summer.* **As the path levels out at the bottom, follow the River Iwerne, a tributary of the Stour, back into Stourpaine.**

5. **At the end of the track past some houses, turn left along the lane. Ignoring Coach Lane on the left, go straight ahead and back to the church. From here, retrace the outward route back over the several arms of the Stour and the millpond to the A357. Cross the road.**

6. **This time, turn up the lane by the war memorial, passing Durweston Farmhouse and Manor Court, then right at the T-junction and back to the car.**

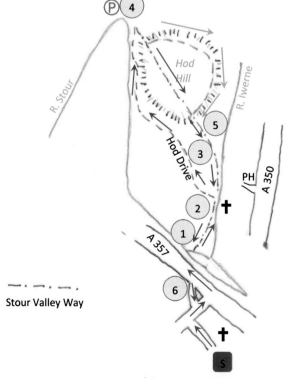

Stour Valley Way

84

RAMBLE 19 – Child Okeford and Hambledon Hill

5 ¾ miles

A truly beautiful walk but not for the faint-hearted; Hambledon Hill is steeper then its brother Hod so it's not for dodgy knees! (You can, of course, walk round one of the lower levels of the hill, but you won't get the views). There is a choice of routes over the top – you may find an OS map (or similar) useful here. Equally, although the earlier part of the walk follows the Stour Valley Way/ St. Edward's Way (SEW), not all the signage has been well-maintained and the route is therefore somewhat patchy. As regards refreshment, there is a shop and also two pubs in Child Okeford, (the Baker Arms and the Saxon Inn), tea at Shillingstone Station on Wednesdays and weekends in the summer (check times) or a picnic up on the hill. Maps: BFCM, 118.

GETTING THERE: Leave Blandford going north on the A350. After about a mile take a left-hand turn onto the A357 signposted Sturminster Newton. After going through Shillingstone, and not far past the station, park on the right after having taken the sign to Child Okeford. **Leave the car park by walking under the railway bridge then cross the road and follow Trailway sign.**

1. Almost immediately, go over a stile on the right, following the route of the St. Edward's Way (this is a pilgrimage route from Shaftesbury to Wareham) diagonally across the field. At the other side of the field go through a gateway over a small bridge onto a track between fields to another bridge. Follow the footpath direction and soon walk with stream on right. Cross the stream by a large willow tree near a water outlet, and carry on following the route through several more fields and gates, making for some houses away to the right. At the end of this section, walk beside a line of young oak trees up to another gate and out onto a track at the end.

2. Turn right and out onto the road; opposite is a road called Jacob's ladder. Walk left up the "main" road to a T-junction at the war memorial. *Child*

Okeford is a thriving village whose population is increasing rather then falling, with a shop and PO, doctor's surgery, two pubs and a modernised but attractive church where Sir Arthur Sullivan conducted the first performance of "Onward Christian Soldiers". Notable inhabitants have been Sir John Tavener and Duncan Sandys MP (both of whom are buried in the churchyard), the 16th century radical vicar William Kethe who wrote several well-known hymns including "All People That On Earth Do Dwell" and "All Worship The King", (but who spent some years exiled in Switzerland on account of his brand of Protestantism) and Sooty and Sweep (lodging with Harry Corbett until his death in

1989). It also played its part in the Liberation of Europe in 1945, being used by the US army as billets for its troops; "Whites only" of course, the black soldiers had to make do with Shillingstone!

3. Cross the road and walk up a NO THROUGH ROAD towards the church. Walk to right of church through both the graveyards and out onto the drive to the Manor. Turn right, then soon left through a gate into a field, following a footpath sign. Walk down the first side of field (hedge to left) . As you continue along the second side you are rejoining SEW. At the end,

out through a metal gate and then almost immediately right through a wooden one onto a protected path uphill between trees.

4. Where this track ends the NT enclosure of Hambledon Hill begins. There is a map on a panel board. The routes over the top of the hill are many and varied, but the best views, of course, are from the highest points. Generally, aim for the top then stay on the ridge on the left-hand side, walking in a SSE direction. Aim for the trig point situated on the bridleway which has a fence alongside it. *Hambledon Hill is one of a line of Iron Age hill forts occupied by Vespasian and the Second Augusta in 44 AD. Excavations have revealed both a Neolithic ceremonial burial site and an Iron Age hillfort. It rises to 190m above sea level and has unrivalled views over the Stour valley and Cranborne Chase in an Area of Outstanding Natural Beauty. During the English Civil War, many ordinary people, particularly farmers and the clergy, became incensed with both sides owing to the destruction and pillaging, and formed associations to resist both Royalists and Parliamentarians. There were many such groups in this area who occupied the ancient hillforts for protection. They were called "Clubmen" because they had no real military weapons, often only clubs. In 1645 Cromwell persuaded a large band in Shaftesbury to disperse, but about 2,000 re-grouped on Hambledon Hill. Inadvisedly, when they were invited to disperse again, they fired on the Roundheads killing several, who then retaliated, attacked them, finally rounding them up and imprisoning them initially in Iwerne Minster church. Thus ended the Clubmen's Last Stand. Later on, General Wolfe used it as a training camp for his soldiers in attacking uphill – obviously successful as put into use in scaling the heights of Abraham to take Quebec from the French in 1759.*

5. At the trig point turn right through a gate and bear diagonally right over the field, in the direction of the village to reach the start of a track which continues down, skirting the edge of Hambledon Hill and its ramparts with a fence on the right to a gate. Go through gate and carry on down to reach

a kissing-gate on the right and a NT sign and notice board. Continue left here, down the track to reach road at Markstone Cottages.

6. Turn left onto road.
7. After several hundred yards turn right onto a NO THROUGH ROAD where you can see a house to the left whose end timbers are painted brown. Where metalled road fizzles out at Chisel Farmhouse/Little Hanford, follow a bridleway right (also Dairy House deliveries). Soon continue left on bridleway, now on a wide track downhill between fields. At the end of this track there is an unclear footpath sign – the route goes through a gate into the middle field (the second field from the left). Follow footpath along right-hand side of field, through a gap into next field, making for the Wilson-Haines bridge which crosses the Stour at this point.
8. Cross bridge, then turn left to shortly reach Trailway through a wide metal gate. Turn right, passing Shillingstone station and back to car.

Shillingstone Station was a stop on the old Somerset and Dorset Railway (see Rambles 13 and 18) and there is an ongoing project to restore it to its former glory. In summer, there is a café and shop open on Wednesdays and at weekends.

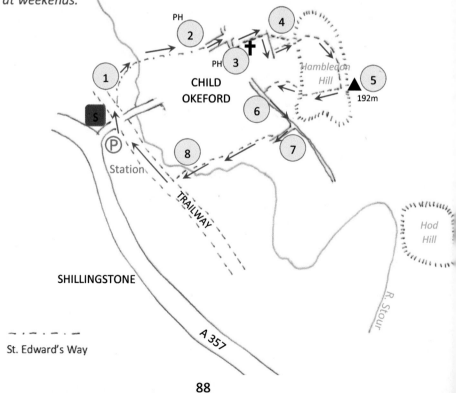

RAMBLE 20 – Fontmell Down and Melbury Beacon

4 miles or 3 miles without Beacon

A short but challenging walk which mainly consists of an initial descent and ends with the climb up to the Beacon. There are beautiful views over the Stour Valley and the villages of Compton Abbas and Melbury Abbas. Much of it is on NT land and there is a short distance on quiet lanes so generally good for dogs, although some areas where they may have to be on leads due to livestock. Refreshment opportunities exist at the café at Compton Abbas Airfield and of course there are plenty of beautiful places to picnic. Maps: 118.

This area of chalk upland has been gradually purchased by the NT in memory of Thomas Hardy who walked these hills in the latter part of the 19th century and, as the information boards in the car park explain, this is a wildlife-rich area, from the spring flowers and orchids (for which the grassland is famous) to the many varieties of butterflies in the summer. Birdlife, too, is varied and in recent years red kites have established a presence here. On the opposite side of the road, Compton Abbas Airfield is not only an interesting aviation experience but has a café with an outside terrace for watching take-offs and landings. It had a brief moment of notoriety in 1993 when the disgraced businessman Asil Nadir escaped from the boys in blue by piloting himself from here to Cyprus (no extradition treaty).

GETTING THERE: Leave Blandford on the C13 (Shaftesbury Lane) as far as the sign for Compton Abbas Airfield (Gore Clump). A little further on, on the left, is a small parking area. If full, there is room for several more cars a bit further on or, alternatively, take the first turning on the right to the airfield where there is some road parking. **There is an information board in the main car park and the walk starts by going through the gate here and following the path straight ahead and gently downhill across the down with the fence to the left. There are other paths going off to the left but ignore them and continue ahead going downhill. This is Clubmen's Down.** *(For more on the Clubmen, see RAMBLE 19).*

1. After about ¾ mile, go through a gate, leaving NT land. At the end of the trees on the right, come out into a field and follow the marked pathway down to the right and through a gate. Continue to another gate (ignoring a footpath to the left) and then onto a path between hedges and out onto a lane. *The little village of Compton Abbas (Compton from Saxon words for a village in a narrow valley and Abbas signifying that it was once owned by Shaftesbury Abbey) lies nestled between the hills. It is more accurately the twin villages of East and West Compton. The current church was built in 1866 as the focus of the village moved to the west, but the ruined 15th century tower of the earlier one can be visited on the walk.*

2. Turn right here and follow the lane round to the right and up through the village, ignoring any roads on the left. At a T-junction turn right and continue ahead to the ruined church of St. Mary's (postbox in the wall). If at this point Melbury Beacon seems a step too far there is an option of taking a road going downhill (initially) on the right which is "Unsuitable for motor vehicles". After about 100 yards the track turns left, going past a house. It then becomes rougher and starts climbing back to the car park which is reached in about a mile. (There is also a NT entrance to Fontmell Down as you climb, on the right.)

3. Soon after the lane has turned left, take a wide track on the right which leads to a gate and into a field. Follow this bridleway to the end of the field.

4. Go through a gate on the right which re-enters NT land, Melbury Hill. There are now several choices about how to get up to Melbury Beacon (ahead and to the left). Either climb the hill by any route or, alternatively, follow the track diagonally right uphill and onto a wide chalky track, still going right uphill. Then, after several hundred yards, take any of the small pathways uphill and off to the left, aiming for a gate in the fence which runs along the top. (The most important consideration is to reach the fence line above and then follow it left, uphill, to the beacon.)

5. Do not go through the gate, but turn left along the fence line and then do the final ascent to the Beacon. This one, too, served as a communication site in 1588 and subsequently in the Napoleonic wars.

6. Retrace steps back downhill as far as the gate mentioned in 5. This time, go through the gate and then go right, walking with the fence to the right, up and then down, to the road.

7. Go through the gate and then use the protected path right back to the car park.

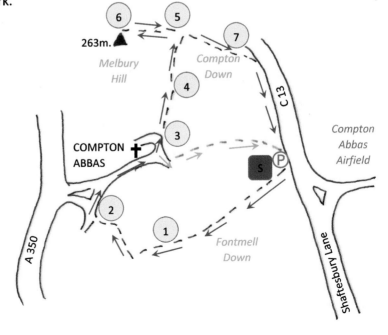